About the author

Ladislau Dowbor was educated in Brazil before being forced abroad following the 1964 coup. He studied Political Economy at the University of Lausanne in Switzerland and obtained his doctorate in Economics from the Central School of Planning and Statistics in Warsaw. He spent much of his life as a consultant with several United Nations agencies and is currently a Professor at the Pontifical Catholic University of São Paulo. He is the author of numerous books on economic and social development, available at http://dowbor.org

About this book

Ladislau Dowbor is a renowned Brazilian economist. He has been closely involved in recent years with President Lula's PT administration in Brazil, as well as with the World Social Forum movement. His work as an economic adviser has taken him to many different parts of the world, working for the United Nations among others, and in countries as diverse as Poland, Portugal, Guinea-Bissau, post-Soviet Mongolia, Sandinista Nicaragua and democratic South Africa.

This remarkable book – part autobiographical reflection, and part summation of the key conclusions he has reached over a lifetime concerned with economics and society – is a wise and deeply humane account. He is cogently critical of the narrowness of conventional economics in both its moral blindness and its distance from any genuine concern with actual people's lives. At the same time, he rejects old-fashioned statist economics as well as utopian 'post-economics' ideas of social organization. Instead, from his experience he has drawn richly detailed and thoroughly practical conclusions about economic and social policy. The approaches and principles he enunciates are of abiding relevance to all developing countries as they seek new policies to replace the neoliberal, market-fixated prescriptions that have delivered neither growth, nor social justice, nor environmental sustainability.

Economists, development specialists, social activists, political leaders and policy makers around the world all have a huge amount to learn from this humane, wise and practical thinker and activist.

The Broken Mosaic
For an Economics Beyond Equations

Ladislau Dowbor

Foreword by
Hazel Henderson

Translated by
Mark Lutes

Zed Books
LONDON AND NEW YORK

The Broken Mosaic: For an Economics Beyond Equations was first published
in English by Zed Books Ltd, 7 Cynthia Street, London N1 9JF, UK and
Room 400, 175 Fifth Avenue, New York, NY 10010, USA in 2005
www.zedbooks.co.uk

First published in Portuguese by Editora Vozes Ltda, Rua Frei Luis 100,
25689-900, Petrópolis, RJ, Brazil in 2000.

Cover designed by Andrew Corbett
Set in 11/14.5 pt Garamond by Long House, Cumbria, UK
Printed and bound in Malta by Gutenberg Press Ltd

Distributed in the USA exclusively by Palgrave Macmillan, a division of
St Martin's Press, LLC,175 Fifth Avenue, New York, NY 10010

A catalogue record for this book is available from the British Library

US Cataloging-in-Publication Data is available from the Library of Congress

ISBN 1 84277 632 0 (cased)
ISBN 1 84277 633 9 (limp)

Contents

Foreword
Hazel Henderson

It is a privilege to offer my thoughts on the work of Ladislau Dowbor and the publication of this book. Dowbor is one of those rare scholars and even rarer economists who engage in a deeply experiential personal exploration of what is abstractly termed 'economic development'. I promise you that this is the most non-boring, positively exciting book on cutting-edge economic thinking that you will ever hope to read!

Dowbor's impressive credentials and many previous books whet our appetite for his wonderful weaving of the professional and the personal in this volume. Among the brilliant insights into the way the discipline of economics is evolving, Dowbor shares the often painful stories of political persecution, imprisonment and exile he suffered along the way.

From his birth in France in 1941 to Polish parents who fled from the Germans, Dowbor's life was caught up in the tides of war. In 1951, his family reached Brazil, where his engineer father had a contract with a steel plant owned by Luxemburgers in Minas Gerais. His mother, a doctor, cared for Ladislau and his brother in Belo Horizonte, where he studied at the Colégio Loyola. His father moved to Recife after his mother returned to live in Poland. Young Ladislau joined his father and became a reporter on a Recife newspaper.

Today, Ladislau Dowbor is one of the key intellectual voices in the emerging powerhouse that is Brazil. Emblematic of Brazil's creativity and new intellectual vigour is the World Social Forum, birthed in 1999 in the gracious city of Porto Alegre. This annual gathering of global civic society challenges the sterile 'Washington Consensus' model of economics promoted by the world's tired, increasingly worried elites that frequent the World Economic Forum in Davos, Switzerland.

The World Social Forum sprang from a group of Brazilian thinkers, writers, politicians, labour leaders and business chiefs who forged the coalition that brought President Lula to power. They include Tarso Genro, who as mayor of Porto Alegre supported and hosted the World Social Forum, thus helping to make his city famous and a chic tourist destination; Oded Grajew, the visionary business leader whose successful toy company launched his philanthropic work for Brazil's children; Candido Grzybowski, civic leader of the Rio-based IBASE; and many other leaders of the Workers Party (PT), including intellectuals Paul Singer, Ladislau Dowbor and Roberto Savio, founder of InterPress Service.

As you read this book, you will find the many threads that are weaving the new ideas, policies and visions of 'Another World is Possible', the movement now finding a global platform in sunny Porto Alegre at the World Social Forum.

Ladislau Dowbor has always worked to expand economic models into the full systems thinking that is needed to address the issues of the world's dynamic, evolving societies. He and I welcome the new opening that occurred after the 2004 Nobel Prize awards, as the Central Bank of Sweden was forced to acknowledge that its million dollar prize, set up in 1969 to legitimize neoclassical economics, had been exposed by none other than Alfred Nobel's heir, Peter Nobel.

This Bank of Sweden Prize in Economic Sciences in Memory of Alfred Nobel (its real name) was never contemplated by Nobel. The prize had become an embarrassment to the Nobel Foundation and many real Nobel Prize winners. In my interview with Peter Nobel, he stated 'The Bank of Sweden, like a cuckoo, has placed its egg in the nest of another very decent bird. This is infringing the Nobel name and trademark.' Nobel added that the Bank's Prize sought to legitimize a narrow group of people who developed economic models to speculate in stock markets and options – the opposite of the goals of Alfred Nobel.

A chorus of mathematicians, physicists, psychologists and historians of science has since gone public to emphasize that economics is not a science, but a profession in need of higher standards of public accountability. Ladislau Dowbor and many other comprehensive thinkers welcome these clarifications, since they empower other disciplines, marginalized groups and new voices in public policy debates.

It seems that Dowbor is one of those rare people who are able to learn useful lessons from every one of life's experiences. This explains his approach to teaching economics, as I have witnessed as a guest lecturer in his courses at the famous Catholic University of São Paulo.

While you read the extraordinary story of Dowbor's life in these pages, you will understand how his brand of economics developed its deeply ethical core. Only someone who thoroughly empathizes with the plight of street children or hard-working people living in grinding poverty can see through and expose the academic sophistries of most neoclassical economic theories.

I have been most impressed by Dowbor's books, always aiming to empower people with a deeper knowledge of the sometimes absurd assumptions economists make about the world. Sitting around the dinner table in Ladislau and Fátima Dowbor's capacious kitchen, with his wonderful family and grandchildren, is an intellectual and gustatory feast. Listening to Dowbor explain to me some of the subtleties of Brazilian society from his house overlooking the miles of twinkling lights of São Paulo was a rare treat.

Like Dowbor, I have come to love Brazil and its warm, creative, clever and hard-working people. I have been fortunate to be an invited lecturer since 1993 at São Paulo's famed private management and leadership institute, Amana-Key Desenvolvimento & Educação, headed by the brilliant Oscar Motomura. Thanks to this association, three of my own books have been published in Brazil by Editora Cultrix of São Paulo. I have seen at first hand the rising power and influence of Brazil, with its 180 million people living in this sprawling land roughly the size of the United States of America.

With the election of President Luis Inácio Lula da Silva in 2001, Brazil is making huge strides, not only as one of the world's top ten industrial powers, but in its new social policies addressing hunger, poverty and the distribution of land to landless peasant farmers. Much remains to be done as Brazil's new leaders forge their own unique path to human development.

I recall participating with Ladislau in a ground-breaking conference held in Curitiba in October 2003, co-organized by two of our colleagues – Thais Corral of the Rio-based civic leadership group REDEH and Rosa Alegria, one of Brazil's best-known 'futurists' and President of the São Paulo-based Perspektiva. Co-organizing and hosting this same International Conference on Implementing New Indicators of Sustainability and Quality of Life (ICONS) was another close friend, Rodrigo Loures, president of the leading business group in the State of Paraná. This kind of cutting-edge collaboration and creativity is typical of Ladislau Dowbor. In a report on the conference for my syndicated column 'Statisticians of the World Unite', I described the huge advances made by Brazilian statisticians and others from around the world in redefining wealth and progress beyond economics and GDP growth.

As Europe, China, Japan and India all continue to deepen their alliances with Brazil, this book offers a panoramic, loving, sometimes critical view of its contemporary history and prospects for the future. I enjoyed this book immensely and am delighted that my friend Robert Molteno and Zed Books are bringing it to readers worldwide.

Enjoy!

St Augustine, Florida
January 2005

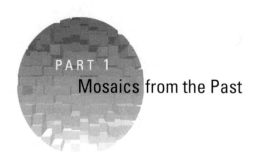

PART 1
Mosaics from the Past

Economics helps to shape our vision of the world, but it alone cannot be our world view. The economic dimension represents only one aspect of what we are. The explanatory strength of this dimension, however, comes from the fact that power and the dynamics of social transformation are structured in great part around economic interests. Anyone who doesn't understand economic processes will fail to understand elementary things such as why we are capable of feats such as travelling to the moon, but are incapable of avoiding the tragedy of the eleven million children who die annually from hunger and other absurd causes, or of reducing the planetary rate of environmental destruction.

Understanding the economy is only partially a technical process. The way we see the world is influenced not only by our capacity for technical analysis and theoretical perspectives, but also by a mixture of emotional experiences, of things that happen in our daily lives and in our social environment. Intellectual processes don't take place in a vacuum. What is truly interesting is not the theoretical developments themselves, but how these interact with the simple dilemmas that all human beings face. Che Guevara once wrote that a politician who doesn't know enough to stop and tie the shoes of a child doesn't understand what life is about. At the real centre of our strange human adventure are values, our individual fragility or generosity, our capacity or impotence in terms of organizing a society that works.

The approach to economics that I present here resembles an autobiography. It is, in fact, a mosaic of experiences made by a person who chose to be an economist, not because he particularly liked economics, but because he understood that without understanding the economy he would not understand other things – the non-economic world.

To write this type of autobiographical economics could appear to be an exercise in narcissism. We are all somewhat given to thinking that our life is interesting. But the real motivation here was the conviction that presenting economics through concrete personal experiences could be more real than another discussion of economic theory.

Beginnings

I was born in France in 1941, to Polish parents, in a gambling house on the Spanish border. It is no doubt very difficult for most people in Brazil to imagine what it was like to be born in Europe in 1941, in the midst of a conflict that killed 60 million persons. We don't choose where we are born. Since Spain at the time had lofty moral standards, the rich went to gamble and have their fun in France, and thus the Franco regime seeded the Pyrenees with casinos along the border. My parents, who had participated in the First World War and thus weren't much moved by the patriotic national anthems of the Second, fled the Germans through the south of Poland and ended up in France, and continued moving south ahead of the German advance. And so I was born in the Pyrenees, on the Spanish border, in a gambling house. Everything has its reasons.

Being born in a foreign country is a defining experience, because one starts off one's life already out of place. Such a child is forced into self-awareness, because children, who react strongly to any difference in clothes, accent or culture, see the foreign child as a choice target. So from an early age cultures are in conflict – nothing is really sponta-neous, natural or obvious, because everything is seen one way at home, and another way on the street. At home it was father and mother, Poland, religion, values; the street and school conveyed another culture, other values. There was no 'natural' value system, but rather the possibility of different values for everything. From a young age, choosing was always a difficult necessity, but also enriching. We are all stuffed full of simplified ideas, which we accept because everyone accepts them, but which fail to withstand the slightest critical appraisal. We'll come back to this.

War is another factor. All of Europe is marked by it, especially by the deep conviction that any man, rich or poor, educated or not, can under particular circumstances become a hero, and under others a beast. After seeing the aberrations that human beings are capable of under certain circumstances, the categories of a 'good man' and 'evil man' lose their value as determinants of behaviour. We could – it is usually easier or more comfortable – simply choose to apply one label or the other. For example, we could think the Israelis are good, and the Palestinians bad, in the Middle East conflict. Or we could choose to be for or against the Serbs in ex-Yugoslavia. When we use this approach, no matter how sophisticated our arguments, the world ends up looking like a more or less complex version of a cops and robbers film. In fact, it is not a matter of who is good or bad: people are a creation of their circumstances. Do we still think the Germans 'are' bad? More important than glorifying the good and persecuting the bad is to think about circumstances, and about the contexts that construct or destroy social relations. Being in a war, from a young age, and experiencing its consequences, leaves profound marks.

In 1951 we arrived in Brazil thanks to a contract that my father, a metallurgical engineer, had signed with the Companhia Siderúrgica Belgo-Mineira, in Minas Gerais. We lived there in the 'Engineers' Village', and it was a shock to me, the first shock I experienced in Brazil, to see a universe so profoundly divided between the rich and the poor, between the *Vila dos Engenheiros* and *Vila Tanque*, where the workers lived. The impression someone arriving from Europe gets is that the division between *Casa Grande* and S*enzala*, which dominated the sugar plantations during the slave economy, is still present, no matter how much modern technology has been introduced. And another idea took shape, which I would become aware of later, that modernity means an appropriate form of human relations, and not an abundance of machines or cars. The residents of Alfaville, an expensive gated community near São Paulo, may like their island of tranquillity. Some think it means they've gotten somewhere, while others are aware of the absurdity of it. Those living outside the walls of Alfaville already call their neighbourhood *Alfavela* (*favela* = shanty town). Does this kind of modernization really lead anywhere?

My father never liked the authoritarianism of the Luxemburgers who owned the sprawling steel plant at Monlevade. One day he revealed to me a simple way to improve productivity in the steel rolling plant, by correcting a structural error. I asked him what the management thought, and he looked at me with astonishment, because he would not communicate it to the management – it wasn't in his interest. His attitude made a strong impression on me, because it appeared obvious to me that if you see a way to improve something, you will do something about it. From my father's perspective, the plant was 'theirs', the other side of the fence, another world. Thus engineers in a company are simultaneously inside and outside, they meet their obligations and receive their salary, but nothing more. Each side only fulfils its obligations. One day he took the side of a worker in a dispute with a German engineer, and shortly thereafter he was looking for work in São Paulo. The plant also divided the world into 'us' and 'them'. Those divisions were not an invention of Karl Marx.

While my father made arrangements in São Paulo, we stayed in Belo Horizonte, where I studied at Colégio Loyola, and lived in the district of Gameleira. My mother was a doctor. One day, on Afonso Pena Avenue, a woman with a clearly undernourished baby in her arms approached her to ask for money. My mother took one look at the child and started making a huge scene, and wouldn't stop until someone called a doctor, an ambulance, anything. Aged 11 at the time, I was mortified, and tried to pull my mother away by the arm. But that's the way she was – she wouldn't tolerate the intolerable, and had no fear of a scandal. Some things just aren't acceptable. To this day, twenty years after her death, I still feel a little bit of her strength. In fact, for a woman to become a doctor in the 1920s, she had to be some woman.

My mother's solidity wasn't sufficient to allow her to adapt to life in Brazil. Or perhaps her capacity for indignation was too great. After Stalin's death, she decided to return to Poland, to make preparations for her family's return. But the family never returned. As an indirect effect of the war, the part of the family still in Brazil became more absorbed in local life, while she was being reabsorbed by her family in Poland. Since my father worked in companies located far from urban centres, my brother and I, both teenagers and already living in São Paulo, learned to enjoy the liberties of city life – the street-corner scene, bars, neighbourhood football games – all the benefits of loose urban existence that compensated for the loss of a structured family life. The cultural richness of Brazil was quickly swallowing up any remaining European vestiges, as it has done for so many generations of immigrants. People are just people, wherever they come from.

Emotions work in mysterious ways. I fell desperately in love with a Jewish girl, of Polish origins like myself. When her father discovered that she was hanging out with a *goy*, he quickly sent her off to Israel, where she might be able to meet Jewish boys. Europe and its hatreds were carried to Brazil, where they hit us with a violence we had not imagined. Her father had lost his family in Poland, and he couldn't accept that his daughter hadn't inherited his hatreds. I worked for an entire year – it was 1963 – trying to pull enough money together to go find her in Israel, at a time when travelling to Europe was considered a big thing. Since my father worked at Açonorte, in the state of Pernambuco, I went to work in the city of Recife, where I became a reporter for the *Diário da Noite* and the *Jornal do Comércio*.

I wrote well, and soon the paper assigned me to cover the sugar cane plantations. When I went to the association of plant owners to introduce myself and gather information, they offered me twice the amount of money I made from the paper. They explained that it was normal and that the paper had done me a favour, because journalists covering the area always received this bonus. I refused the offer, and the editor later joked that some day in the Brazilian press it would be normal to refuse this kind of thing. In fact, it wasn't only the institutionalized corruption that shocked me. Much of the population of Recife lived in grinding poverty, and the effervescence of ideas under the progressive government of Miguel Arraes generated a new cultural dynamic in the city. As a reporter, despite my age, I met Paulo Freire, Celso Furtado, Gilberto Freire, Ariano Suassuna and other figures who in different ways contributed to my reflections about the reality of Brazil and the Northeast. In the Popular Culture Movement I met people my own age who were much more politicized and strongly committed to bringing about social transformations. With my exposure to all these new ideas and points of reference, my taste for philosophy and linguistics shifted to economics. I wanted to understand things, the why's, the mechanisms, and already was convinced that economic dynamics were at the root of social problems.

One night my father, who lived at the Açonorte plant site, came to Recife and invited me out to dinner. We went to eat lobster. At the door of a restaurant was a child who was obviously famished. I ate the dinner out of respect for my father, but the ethical dilemma became crystal clear in my mind: a person who dines on lobster and lets a child go hungry has only two possible paths, either change his or her values and start seeing a luxurious feast in front of a starving child as normal, or try to change the situation that creates these absurdities. With time I would come to learn the complex theoretical constructions that try to show that consuming stimulates the economy, so that my good lunch is the best solution for other people's hunger. Thus selfishness and good conscience are reconciled, egoism and altruism become parts of the same process. It is a beautiful construction, but at the time I didn't know the theories, and young people tend to lack the necessary hypocrisy.

Shortly after this dinner I read a simple and good book: it argued that the charity of a coin on the street is fine, but it is better to create organizations that support the poor, and better still to create fair institutions that prevent poverty from emerging. They are different levels of charity. For me, the ethical direction had become clear, not by reading Karl Marx, but probably by a mixture of common sense, simple Christian roots and values inherited from my mother: poverty is the major scandal, and individual measures are not sufficient.

Another process became clear to me, by exposure to the hard realities of Brazil's Northeast: beyond a certain level of destitution, the poor lose the autonomy to construct their own space in society, and become excluded. This dynamic generates a huge number of people deprived of their capacity to reduce their misery, and for these people, free enterprise and free markets have little meaning. In the game of life, it is understandable that different people are more or less successful. But to play, one needs to have at least the entry ticket – the initial capital, in the form of health, education, money or what have you. It's not a matter of charity. It is simply a matter of the right of human beings to participate in the social game, to get to the starting line. Economics deals with the mechanisms that govern the behaviour of economic agents. And what about those who aren't economic agents?

At the time, of course, this vision was somewhat confused. But gradually the understanding took shape that an economist sitting in his office may rationally consider how people optimize the use of their money, choose between investment in the stock market or in foreign currencies, and so forth, but very rarely brings into his theory the particular situation of the billions of destitute people who have no choice in the matter, but are still human beings. To be 'free to choose', you have to have a choice.

Studies

At the end of 1963 I went to Israel. With US$230 in my pocket, on an Air Portugal flight that offered discounts for journalists, I arrived in Lisbon, and from there hitchhiked to Naples, where I got on an old ship going to Haifa. The ship was full of Jews on their way to visit their new homeland, and the nights echoed with Hebrew songs. After two more days of hitchhiking I was in Eilat, on the Gulf of Aqaba, with Pauline. Life is not a soap opera. Like two blind people we groped around in search of each other, because one year of adolescence is an eternity, and both had matured into two new people who had to reconstruct their relationship. In one year of separation Pauline had not received a single letter of mine that had not been opened, and her father had ordered her passport taken away so she couldn't leave the country. She couldn't leave, and I couldn't stay because I was a tourist, and a non-Jew, with a three-month visa. We learned the harsh reality: society is organized around documents, not around people. And what use is social organization that is not focused on concrete persons?

With the help of friends who were part of a clandestine support network that existed at the time, we went to work on a farm at the edge of the Dead Sea, in Neot-Hakikar. We worked with excellent agronomists, learning to grow tomatoes, date palms and other crops, and to use drip irrigation and other groundbreaking technologies. In the infernal heat of the region, almost 400 metres below sea level, no one asked for documents, and it paid well.

It was there that we heard on the radio the news of the military coup in Brazil in 1964, which deepened our indignation and desire for change. Increasing the minimum wage and giving rural workers land to work, two obvious and not exactly subversive proposals, had been sufficient cause for Brazil's ruling class to resort to a coup. The bridge between economics and politics became clear to me: if you accept the misery of the majority, and thus appear to be a well-behaved people, there will be no problems in maintaining a democracy. But if you threaten to use democracy to redistribute income, a dictatorship is created. In other words, to have access to income, the people need democracy. But to have the right to democracy, you cannot demand an income. Thus was created this curious monster that we have today – a democratic system of economic and social exclusion.

The Israelis discussed with us the tragedy of yet another Latin American military dictatorship, then we went back to work picking tomatoes. Pauline and I were not the only lost souls in this world: working beside us were the Bedouins, who worked in the harvest but did not participate in politics or social life. The Israelis felt sorry for us, who now faced a dictatorship at home, but they didn't see the problems in their own back yard. It's always the others who are wrong.

I learned Hebrew, and was deeply moved by the experience of living in the biblical setting, of going through Scorpion Pass in the Negev desert, and drinking fresh water from Ein Gedi while remembering the words of the Sulamite from the *Song of Songs*: 'A bundle of myrrh is my beloved to me, he shall abide between my breasts. A cluster of cypress my love is to me, in the vineyards of Engaddi'. In the biblical Beersheba, at the edge of the Negev desert, we hung out at a decrepit bar, along with a few disoriented regulars and the last four prostitutes remaining in the region. The bar was eloquently named 'The Last Chance'.

We didn't complain. Being inside the system and participating in the economic rat race had its attractions. Living outside the system also had its appeal, including the romantic element. Wouldn't combining the two be still more appealing? Is there any logic in having to choose between one and the other? It would take me decades to understand that these weren't just idle adolescent musings: marrying economic needs to our human dimension continues to be the essential challenge of the world we are building. Efficiency, if we can't build a world that is agreeable in terms of our concrete day-to-day life, is nonsense. It generates competent technocrats who, when successful, become rich, solitary and frustrated.

I've always liked languages. I learned Polish at home, and later French. Portuguese came naturally with the move to Brazil. I learned English in school, because I liked it, and would go on to learn Spanish, Italian and Russian. Biblical Hebrew came to me because of an absurd situation. Pauline and I were trying to get married, not because we considered it important in itself, but so she could obtain a Brazilian passport (I was already naturalized) and leave the country. To avoid improper intermixing, Israel only allowed religious weddings, and didn't permit weddings between people of different religions. The upshot was that Pauline took catechism classes, while I started visiting a Rabbi at a religious school, and our ingenuous idea was that we would marry in the first religion that gave us the chance. We also explored the idea of both of us converting to Islam, but we lacked the contacts. Some twenty years later, I would discover that my mother had come to know that we were trying to convert to any religion that would allow us to marry, have papers for Pauline and leave Israel, and, as a strong Catholic believer, it made her hysterical. Reason is a shallow layer in most of us. We still study in school how Jews were forced to formally adopt other religions, as if it were some ancient absurdity.

At the same time we made the rounds of the consulates and embassies looking for someone who would put a visa on a temporary document that Pauline had received. Finally a sympathetic Danish Consul, moved by Pauline's situation, gave her a three-month visa under very irregular conditions. This allowed us to get a transit visa for Italy. Pauline had come to hate Israel because of the continuous control she was under there, and desperately wanted to get out and feel free, her own person. To escape from something so prosaic as parental control – switching taxis, in the ridiculous tradition of spy films – we finally embarked from Haifa.

No doubt this all sounds a bit like a soap opera. With a little distance, it's quite striking to see how persons can be deprived of their rights, simply because they don't have the right documents. Or how victims of persecution can become implacable persecutors, victims of racism turn racists. Seeing how European Jews in Israel discriminate against Jews from Africa – called 'blacks' but in fact as white as them – and how they instil in their children racist views of the Arabs, I gradually came to understand how powerful are the emotional and irrational roots of politics. And a sociological point became clear to me: rights, if they are not backed up by organization, do not materialize; they don't exist, however essential they may be. In Italy, we took a picture in front of a Duomo, with pigeons and all, and sent it to Pauline's family in Brazil. Her father stood by his hate. Her mother, I discovered years later, had another reaction: it was winter in Italy, and what she retained from the picture was that Pauline was cold. Women *are* different.

Things aren't easy. Italy did not allow her to stay, and she had to use the Danish visa. We had to pay for a flight to Copenhagen, for Switzerland and Germany refused her a transit visa to go by train. This drained the little money we had, and I went to Lausanne where I could get a job working on trains. Once a month, I took a few days off, and hitchhiked all the way through Germany to Lübeck, and across to Copenhagen, where she was staying with the family of a friend we had met in Israel. Hitchhiking on the autobahns during winter is not a merry experience. A day or two together, and then all the way back....

After some time, the family finally decided to admit our relationship, and invited Pauline back to Brazil. She refused to go unless they sent her a passport and a return ticket. Zero confidence in her own family. Finally, she received the passport, was free to come and go, to travel and cross borders. We are speaking of the 'Free World'. We settled in Lausanne, in Switzerland, trading the Dead Sea for Lac

Leman, with stately swans and a university that accepted foreign students as if it were normal, without the bloody struggle for the best to enter and become a 'success'.

The Lausanne School was well known in the world of economics, and trained fine bankers in the best tradition of Walras and Pareto. It was a good neoclassical school, with a strong focus on history, law, mathematics and theory. I'm not sure which is more valuable – the culture one learns in a new country, or the formal studies. At any rate, today I understand that it is essential to experience a range of countries, not least so that the theoretical analysis itself can have different experiences on which to build. And these experiences can vary widely, depending on cultures and traditions. I am convinced that much of the tendency to use simplified theoretical models in economics is linked to insufficient knowledge of social diversity on the part of the theorists. Trying to understand the economy without understanding society doesn't bear very good fruit. The Washington Consensus can only be a consensus in Washington.

I learned the basics, and got a degree in political economy. I began to understand things, and the more I understood the more irritated I got. Simple things, like the Treaty of Versailles, which at the end of the First World War divided the Middle East into peoples with political capacity, and others that required the tutelage of England and the other great powers. The known oil reserves happened to lie beneath the peoples requiring tutelage. This is an institutionalized cynicism, always accompanied by sophisticated scientific arguments and humanistic motives. Learning about the history of the Vatican removed whatever illusions I may have had about the sanctity of the church. Hitler's military machine had had the solid support of companies like General Motors/Opel and IBM, while most of the large Swiss, French and other banks appropriated the assets of those who disappeared. It is not just a case of past cynicism. Not until 1999 did the Swiss banks start paying back those whose assets had been confiscated, and only after the theft reached the press. The Caisse de Dépôts et Consignations, in France, started returning stolen goods in 2000, also in response to accusations. In the 1990s, General Motors was to receive discreet compensation of hundreds of millions of dollars because its German plant had been bombed by the allies. The plant produced, during the war, engines for German vehicles. Business as usual....

There's nothing like knowing how things work. History is a powerful instrument that allows economic theory to be understood in the real world, and the distinction of valid theoretical arguments from rationalizing rhetoric that simply seeks to justify the interests of the strongest.

At the same time, I started to explore the area of education. I was fortunate enough to encounter Piaget, one of the giants of the theory of knowledge. For his last course, Piaget, already an old man, invited mathematicians, biologists, economists and others to discuss scientific methods. I was one of those invited, thanks in part to Pauline, who studied with him in Geneva. It was striking to see the parallel between the methodologies of Marx in one area, and those of Piaget in another. Rather than measuring intelligence using quantitative methods, as in American IQ tests, Piaget concentrated on the evolutionary process of intelligence. Instead of treating intelligence as an accumulated stock, he saw it as the outcome of a dialectical interaction between the individual and the surrounding world. Rather than a linear evolution, he showed how smaller quantitative changes led to qualitative changes, to structural differences that delimit phases in the evolution of intelligence. It was fascinating, because Piaget bridged the diverse areas of knowledge. It was a defining moment, which drew together my studies of economics with the broader universe of knowledge. I learned the importance of method, and understood that economics is important, but not sufficient.

I read Marx, the new books from the publisher Maspéro, and shared the general indignation with the Vietnam war. Not that this war was worse than the others, but the blatant hypocrisy of the American government made our indignation so much stronger. Looking back, it is impressive how an idea as ridiculously simplified as the Domino Theory was sold to the world, forgetting that the domino pieces were actually countries, and peoples with traditions and history, and deeply differentiated structures and needs. Vietnam changed hands, and no dominoes fell. Bombing North Vietnam was justified by the Tonkin Gulf incident, where the American navy was supposedly attacked by the Vietnamese 'navy' – an absurdity sold as fact by all the traditional media. Decades later, we would face the 'weapons of mass destruction' farce.

The magnitude of the deceptions swept away any vestige of credibility that the United States and the multinationals may have had, and also made us incapable of perceiving any positive elements there might have been. The Americans had their demon – Moscow. And we had ours – the Americans. We thus became in some sense communists, not out of choice, or based on any understanding of what was going on in those countries, but because the ideological polarization pushed anyone who was critical of one side over to the other. If there were so many obvious lies regarding Vietnam, what truth could there be in the accusations against communism? A little reading of history showed that US governments had always supported the brutal dictatorships of Batista, Somoza, Papa Doc, Mobutu, Suharto, the Shah and so many others. We are talking here of millions of deaths, billions of dollars in personal fortunes of dictators, of widespread plundering of national wealth through the alliances of local dictators and transnational corporations with the aid of the government machinery of the US and other rich countries. Defenders of liberty and human rights?

I think that the ethical dimension has always been underestimated. A good number of the young protesters in Europe, as in other continents, received from their parents a healthy supply of domestic appliances and no values. The parents thought they had made enough sacrifices and that their children should be grateful and quiet, but the most generous part of this mass of youth wanted something else. And according to the simplifications that dominated the twentieth century, whoever rebelled in the East was a capitalist lackey, and whoever rebelled in the West was an agent of Moscow. Politics became reduced to the choice between one type of political delinquency and another.

And the corresponding economic theories – planning on the one hand, market on the other – seemed a theoretical gloss that barely covered the underlying brutality: the invisible hand gradually led to the very visible centralized power of large multinational corporations, while the 'actually existing socialism' produced a similar mirror image of centralized economic power, but through the state. And the question, obviously, is not which of the two absurdities is better or worse.

I was in Paris when France stopped, in May 1968. It was very impressive to see the people on the street, the neighbourhoods organizing themselves for direct management of their affairs. It is difficult to reconstruct an abstract but powerful sense, palpable at the time, of people helping each other, of a combination of liberty and solidarity. The feeling swept the planet, from Paris to Woodstock, and even opened some cracks in the dictatorship that was then ruling Brazil. It was as if we had discovered that it was legitimate to have feelings that went beyond the organized and disciplined pursuit of increasing the GNP by a few per cent.

Artists displayed paintings directly on the street, and one talked about everything and nothing with complete strangers. A huge cauldron of pent-up goodwill spilled over, liberating a universe of conviviality, and revealing the frustrated wasteland of lives centred more on money than on life. De Gaulle, startled by the change that was reaching even the police and the army, went to Strasbourg to discuss the potential support of the German army. Faced with a choice between the motherland and the defence of property, the old General knew where his duty lay.

Demonstrations were widespread throughout the world, highlighting the moral bankruptcy of the system. Suddenly, this combination of power and fragility that we faced became transparent. We knew, in a sense, where the evil was, but not where the good was. Because of the polarized context, we supported communism, but it was an artificial by-product of anti-Americanism. Cuba exerted a huge attraction, transparent evidence that finally someone ethical had reached power, with a clearly defined social objective. It wasn't a matter of communist propaganda, claims of the Brazilian security agencies notwithstanding. It was the only decent option in the face of the political injustices, corruption and criminality of the South American regimes. Injustices, corruption and criminality which, incidentally, remain largely intact.

Like so many attempts at social transformation in the twentieth century, Cuba would be a victim of the Cold War: it was consciously forced by the Americans into an extremism that it wasn't seeking, and was adroitly pushed, for its very survival, into the arms of the Soviet Union. There was no room to sit on the fence, the world had to be USA or USSR. Not being pro-American, Cuba had to be pro-Soviet. As pro-Soviet, it was declared a mortal enemy. A relatively small island, isolated in the world, hardened politically by outside aggressions, smothered by the blockade, cannot work. It is an interesting process: the experiment is undermined and, since it proved unviable, it is proven that the model doesn't work. It's as if by pushing the island into the arms of the Soviet Union, one would be proving that communism in general doesn't work. Batista, Somoza, Mobutu – they are friends of democracy. Cuba would be anti-democratic. The Cuban people became a pawn – the important thing was to score points in the great global strategy. Poor Cuba: *Tan lejos de Dios* … and so close to the United States. In this cynical production, the actual interests of the Cuban people never appeared on stage.

A Time to Fight

A group of Brazilian students and professors would meet regularly in Paris. I was paying for my studies by working on the international overnight trains, and would take advantage of the stopovers in Paris to participate in the meetings. The armed struggle didn't seem to me very mysterious; it was in the air, everyone knew of the Vietnamese resistance, the Cuban revolution, the Angolan guerrilla movement, Mozambique, Guinea-Bissau, etc. It was one of the options. Personally, I didn't consider myself capable of any great strategy, because of my age and relative lack of political experience, and when the people I knew in Paris, who had another level of experience, called on me to return to Brazil, I packed my bags and went.

Within two months I was arrested, accused of being a terrorist and a communist. I discovered that I had been sought by the police since the 1964 military coup. I had studied Russian in the Brazil–USSR institute in Recife, which was sufficient proof of subversion, and the lists of people who had studied Russian were published in the newspapers to prove that Brazil was threatened with invasion by dark forces. I didn't get far with the explanation that at the same time I studied American Literature at the Roosevelt Institute, and Italian at the Circolo Italiano, simply out of a love of languages. After some time on the *pau de arara*,[1] electric shocks and a dislocated rib, I had had enough.

---

[1] A horizontal pole from which the victims were suspended during torture.

I invented a story that I had received terrorist messages on the Santa Efigênia Bridge, in a small hiding place in the wall. They agreed to take me to the spot; I tried to jump over the railing and get away, but the rope that they had tied my arms with got caught on the metalwork, and I was left dangling. Back for more electric shocks.

All sorts of characters passed through the third floor of the then DEIC (Departamento de Investigações Criminais). I shared a cell with a young man who had shot a car owner twice, and didn't understand why a person with a .38 at his head failed to obey orders. He was still indignant about it. In the adjoining cell was a young woman. Once in a while a police officer would appear, order her to come to the bars, and touch and abuse her. Someone bothered to explain – she's a whore. These were the forces of law and order. When I was caught, within three minutes they had divided up my watch, money and shoes between them.

I was introduced to all the team on duty. A police officer explained the system to me: if someone was caught, they had to become known to all the officers and were soon released, with the warning that they had to carry money with them at all times in case they met up with any one of them again. If they had no money on them, it was back to the DEIC for another night of *pau de arara* and electric shocks. Thus the criminal came to work for them – the amateur turned professional and acquired a title befitting his new function: he became *administrado*. Since that time, the system has no doubt been modernized. Part and parcel of the economic miracle.

In one week I was released – it was before AI-5,[2] so the other agencies didn't even hear of my imprisonment, and the Police Chief received a wad of money from our political group. They were the forces of order. This time I took up the fight with genuine anger. In a sense, the very torture justified our armed struggle, just as the police and military justified their torture by the fact that we were armed. In the process of polarization, the other is always to blame. It

[2] Ato Institucional N. 5, a coup within the military regime which gave power to the *linha dura*, the hard-liners among the military.

was interesting to become aware of the immense machinery of police, lawyers, journalists, accountants and other professionals that keep the corrupt and violent system of the powerful in working order. They are the cellar rats of any oppressive system. Dirty hands need friendly clean hands, and vice-versa.

The fight was a dramatically unequal one. Not that it was just small groups of students, as some publications tried to show. At this time there were as many as 10,000 people in prisons for political reasons, and 10,000 people willing to risk their lives to change things is no small matter. The general population, when they realize that the climate is becoming dangerous, seek cover. It doesn't mean that they would not like to have social justice, peace and democracy. Who doesn't feel this permanent contradiction between wanting to secure their own comfort and build their lives, and the shock of seeing a poor child on the street? Both impulses are legitimate. It's not a matter of choosing, but of systematically organizing a society where all have their place.

In the following years, we worked mostly to defend ourselves, because the repression itself obliged us to seek resources, save people who were dying in interrogations, and protect networks of solidarity. And the entire communications machine was naturally in the hands of the repressive state and the large economic groups that supported it. The large media outlets would later justify their role by presenting themselves as victims of censorship. It is interesting to read today, thirty years later, the testimony of Mino Carta, one of the journalists who tell the truth about those times:

> The large press is one of the Brazilian embarrassments. It defended the coup of 1964, and the coup within the coup in 1968 [AI-5]. The large press, except for the *Estado de São Paulo*, was never censored. Not the *Folha de São Paulo,* not *O Globo,* not the *Jornal do Brasil.* The *Estado* was censored simply because it was a dissident group within the supporters of the dictatorship, not because it was an adversary or enemy of the coup.

In terms of relations of power, the determining element was the capacity of the regime to generate a new middle class, whose members had access to university, to their own houses, to the recently created capital market. It was 1969, at the height of the 'economic miracle'. Between the moment of the coup (1964) and the emergence of the armed struggle, four years had passed, the time it took for indignation to translate into popular action with some degree of organization. After four years, the movement towards concentration of wealth gave the system a new logic, and generated a temporary but dramatic growth that radically undermined the political base of the movement. What remained was slow and heroic resistance. I moved into a position of leadership, which was no reflection of my merit, because as our companions fell others had to take their places.

I never thought that it was in vain. Some years later, already in exile, I was sought out in Paris by a group of young Brazilians who told me how important it had been to them, in these *anos de chumbo* ('years of lead' – a Brazilian term for the most repressive years of the dictatorship), to know that there were people who fought and died without giving up hope. One day a journalist asked me if I ever regretted it, because it 'didn't work out' – we didn't take power. I think that the issue thus raised is not one of objectives, of a struggle for power, but rather one of causes, which lead to a refusal to accept something. Frantz Fanon was on the mark with what he called the feeling of 'revolt'. Some things simply cannot be accepted – it is a question of dignity, not of results.

Arrested for a second time, I was exchanged for the German Ambassador, and in the wee hours of a June day in 1970, I stepped off a plane with a group of 40 political prisoners at the Dar el-Beida airport in Algiers. I got off the plane in the same state as they had taken me out of prison – no shoes, no documents, with burns from electric shocks that would be filmed by countless news outlets from all over the planet. On the same day arrived King Faisal of Saudi Arabia, on an official visit. The local newspaper, *El Moudjahid*, put the two headlines on the front page – the 40 Brazilian prisoners and the visiting king. The people quickly dubbed us 'Ali Baba and the forty thieves'.

We received a warm welcome from the population, which had recently emerged from a struggle against French occupation. We didn't pay for any taxis, and Algerian families took us in. It was rare to find a family where at least one member had not been killed or tortured. The technology of combining the *pau de arara* and electric shocks was invented there by the French. The Algerians completely identified with us. It's the circumstances that determine one's values. It did not occur to anyone there to call us terrorists, or deluded students; no one reached for any of the other simplifications we try to substitute for real understanding of what happens. The representatives of the Popular Movement for the Liberation of Angola (MPLA) explained their forms of struggle to us, the Vietcong suggested strategies, the Palestine movement explained their predicament, the Black Panthers from the US wanted to learn about the black movement in Brazil, Johnny Makatini discussed with us ways to spring Mandela from prison.[3] With three quarters of the world's wealth in the hands of a group of rich countries, with dramatic struggles to escape from colonialism and underdevelopment, fighting was not a question of extremism: it was a question of decency. The desire for change was widespread.

The need for change was also clear. What were the Portuguese, from the poorest country in Europe, doing trying to control countries ten times their size in other continents? What were the Americans doing in Vietnam? How could international bodies and the rich countries maintain that their hands were clean while supporting the bloodiest dictators, as long as they remained 'friendly'? How could they justify, in this day and age, the traffic in arms as a business like any other, given their capacity to destroy human beings? How could the

[3] Twenty years later, as Secretary to Mayor Luiza Erundina in the 1990s, I welcomed Nelson Mandela when he made an official visit to São Paulo, and he laughed at the story. For how many decades had the mainstream press presented him as a terrorist? In 2002, I met Ahmed Ben Bella, the first president of independent Algeria, in the Porto Alegre World Social Forum, and was able to thank him for the hospitality the Algerians showed us in the 1970s. The French always presented him as a terrorist. Rather than sticking a 'terrorist' tag on a person or a political movement, it is more helpful to understand that it is dangerous to close all doors to people who want their place in the sun alongside others. When eventually the political changes are made, these people are not terrorists anymore.

single party in Cuba be presented as a dictatorship while the single party in Mexico was regarded as a champion of democracy – not to mention the dozens of other outright dictatorships supported by the rich countries? What right did multinational corporations have to finance the toppling of governments? There was at the time, of course, a marvellous justification for everything – the communist threat.

One thing became clear to me: one barbarity does not justify another, and the very concept that the ends justify the means, so common in communist countries, was a barbarity. In Brazil, Bishop Dom Sigaud justified torture by saying that 'you don't extract information with candy'. The dictatorship imposed a constitution with no consultation and one jurist came out with this gem: 'the revolution creates its own legality'. The CIA financed its operations with cocaine and heroine, explaining that it was necessary to have secret sources of funds. The Israeli Mossad has become a byword for horror. The reality is that the means corrupt and deform the ends.

At the heart of our dilemma, now refugees in Algeria, was a clear awareness and outrage about the way things worked, and our limited capacity to change them. At the same time, we understood that the huge mass of people who struggled for social progress, of which we were a part, constituted an important force for change. The deaths of Martin Luther King, of Marighela, of Lumumba, of Allende, of Amilcar Cabral, of Gandhi and of so many others were not in vain; the part of humanity with the capacity for indignation had at times endured temporary setbacks, but in the long run its witness had allowed historic advances like the end of slavery, social progress for blacks in the United States, decolonization, progress for women, and the organization of workers. The path that was now closed to us was not that of the struggle and its objectives, but rather the vision that social progress could be achieved through short cuts or fast tracks, which would allow political gains without the corresponding foundations in the social and political culture of the population.

In 1972 a meeting was held in Santiago on the question of continuing the armed struggle. I proposed to dissolve the organization, and to reorganize it on the basis of pursuing a new and broader kind of political struggle against the dictatorship. The forces for and against were evenly balanced, but the proposal was defeated. It was patently clear to me that the vote to continue the armed struggle was based more on emotion than on reason, and especially on feelings of guilt that we were safe in another country while others were dying in Brazil. It is difficult to condemn that, because no one acts on pure reason. But it was important for me to understand that a political group – and later I would see that it is also the case with religious and even scientific groups – could create a kind of virtual reality, speaking its own vocabulary, and lose contact with the real world.

The struggle went on. Pauline, who had come to join me in Algeria, was sent to Recife, to try to save a threatened group. She died along with them. She had entered the struggle when I was leaving it, and we were already distant. Not in terms of sentiments, but because of the very madness and tension of the times. Pauline died under torture. The government said she was a 'terrorist', which explains and justifies anything.

Poland

I was of Polish descent, but had not been born in Poland and had never been there. There was a great attraction, and I had always thought it important to make peace with the past, and to get to know my roots. After years of living underground and of being socially uprooted, I felt a powerful need for normality, for feeling a common person. When you belong to a struggling minority, whatever the legitimacy of the process, you tend to create clandestine networks, and end up meeting and talking to persons in a similar situation, gradually generating a self-perpetuating style of life, values and behaviour. A friend you saw in the morning may have been caught in the afternoon; he or she may be dead, or undergoing torture, which makes you rush to protect other persons who may be threatened. Social isolation tends to perpetuate itself, and since all the doors out of the process are closed, you are just pushed deeper into the underground. Being out of Brazil, and formally a refugee, allowed me to get back to the surface.

As my parents were both Polish, I asked the government for papers. At the time I was travelling on an Algerian refugee passport, which was curious, because Algerian papers already suggested terrorism to the so-called normal person, so that Algerian refugee papers were looked upon as downright dangerous.

I also had a great interest in the political and economic organization of the kind of state socialism Poland represented, this surrealistic mixture of communism, militant Catholicism and Russian influences.

I wanted to understand, to go beyond the idiotic 'good' and 'evil' simplifications.

I moved to Poland, returning to a kind of normal life, and started rebuilding my world. I was again with my mother, who was now an elderly woman, but as lively and combative as ever. She thought the consumerist hysteria of the wealthy countries was pathological, and would say to communist party members that communism was great because it protected Poland from economic progress. The authorities were confused, and it made her very satisfied. I also met my brother, Mario, who had returned from Brazil to study at the polytechnic school in Warsaw, met a sweet Polish girl and ended up staying. Our choices are usually not very ideological.

I married Fátima, the daughter of Paulo Freire, who was also a Brazilian refugee at that time. Paulo was in Geneva, working for the World Council of Churches. Fátima was as lost as I with her repeated exiles, but had an impressive capacity for keeping both feet on the ground. I had found my anchor.

Fátima was part of an earlier generation of exiles. Paulo Freire, who had dared to teach literacy in his native impoverished northeast region of Brazil – sufficient proof in itself of communist tendencies – was arrested and later exiled. For Fátima, leaving Brazil in 1964 at the age of 15 meant abandoning her friendships, her extended family, her youthful flings, and school. In Chile, Paulo Freire helped to develop adult education programmes, and was then invited to lecture at Harvard. Later he went to Geneva, always as an exile, without even a Brazilian passport, and advised several governments on their literacy programmes. Fátima and the rest of the family went along. In each country it was necessary to reconstruct friendships, one's social life, and affective relationships that had already been broken so many times. It wasn't easy. We probably read our loss in each other's eyes. The recognition was spontaneous and immediate.

Poland issued me a passport, which I was not to use for subversive purposes. And they gave me a scholarship, which I was able to supplement by teaching languages in different institutions. The kaleidoscope turned again, and I was back studying, trying to understand social processes and to reconstruct my vision of the world. In Lausanne I had studied the neoclassical approach. Now I was seeing the world from another perspective, along the lines of Oskar Lange, Kalecki and other authors whose thoughts went beyond profit. Since I spoke the language, I had no difficulties.

I completed the graduate course in national planning, which involved Poles, Africans, Indians and others in discussing systems of economic organization. There was much discussion of the specific conditions of development with an unlimited labour supply; of choices between advanced and alternative technologies, of the experiences of Poland, India and the Middle Eastern countries, and so on. The theoretical foundations were provided by the works of Michael Kalecki. Having a background in neoclassical thought, I was struck by the fact that the two approaches were more complementary than contradictory. Managing the day-to-day affairs of a mature economy, as in the developed countries, is different from structuring the long-term options of an economy while it is under construction.

I reread the classics, and saw that Adam Smith is much more progressive than the simplistic and absurd caricature that liberalism has turned him into, and that Marx is much more prudent about the alternatives than communism proclaimed. It wasn't a question of 'in practice theory doesn't work'. In fact, in the words of Pawel Sulmicki, a Polish economist, 'there is nothing more practical than a good theory'. This rereading, which many were doing at the time, was part of the confused feeling that the theoretical foundations themselves weren't providing solid footing. Everyone was seeking reformulations, even though the academic establishment put strict limits on anything that could affect the paradigms. It reminded me of the medieval discussions: you could bring new ideas, as long as they were Aristotelian. This difficulty continues to the present day: it appears as a treason to disagree with authors that first gave us ideological legitimacy. The result is the tireless repetition of increasingly surreal slogans, both by the left and the right, while reality demands new approaches.

I was amazed by the richness of the library of the Central School of Planning and Statistics of Warsaw, where I studied. I found there the works of Celso Furtado, Caio Prado Júnior, Roberto Simonsen and many other Brazilians, along with older works like those of Antonil. Years later I encountered Orlando Valverde at the Pontifical Catholic University (PUC) in São Paulo, and mentioned to him how much I enjoyed reading his works on the coffee plantation economy when I was in Warsaw. Touched, very old but lively, he turned to his wife. 'Look, they read Brazilian works in Poland. And when will our universities be so open-minded?'

I decided to study the economic history of Brazil systematically – to learn the facts. The result of this work was my doctoral dissertation, *A formação do capitalismo dependente no Brasil (The formation of dependent capitalism in Brazil)*. This was essentially a methodological analysis, a reorganization of the facts studied and analysed by the classics, but through the theoretical framework of the theories of Samir Amin, Christian Palloix, André Gunder Frank and the Latin American authors linked to dependency theory. The dissertation was later published in Poland, France, Portugal and Brazil. In essence, I came to understand that we need to transcend the oversimplifications that present Brazil as either a poor passive victim of imperialism, or as an independent giant. The complex interaction of underdeveloped economies with the dominant economies is the central theoretical problem. Today this problematic of subaltern participation in the world system has come back to the fore, in the context of the current phase of globalization.

Certain problems appeared never to leave me alone. The Brazilian embassy left Fátima without her passport, and with no documents she couldn't leave Poland, even to visit her family in Geneva. At the same time they informed the Polish government that she was not a refugee, and that they would give her the passport, after the bureaucratic process had run its course. After two and a half years of bureaucratic process and no passport, the Polish government was convinced that in practice Fátima was a political refugee, and based on our marriage and on our Polish son Alexandre, who was born in Warsaw, they gave her Polish citizenship. We were citizens again. And I, as a Doctor of Economics, was no longer a subversive, but a person of progressive ideas.

The three years in Poland were incredibly rich, both in terms of the theoretical and economic history studies of Brazil it had allowed me, and in terms of the practical knowledge of the gigantic bureaucratic mess this version of socialism has created. It certainly was a mess, but much less of a mess than Brazil. But most of all, I discovered how deep the economic, political and cultural roots can go in a country, and how the formal structure can be 'digested' so as to create different realities.

Poland had discovered countless extremely effective arrangements. Service cooperatives, which made available to small farmers extremely decentralized and flexible forms of credit, technical assistance, primary marketing, storage capacity and rental of machinery, worked well because they were managed by the farmers themselves, and contributed greatly to productivity, which contradicts all the claims for economies of scale in this area. On the other hand, state-run agriculture was a disaster. Since 80 per cent of the land was in the hands of small farmers, overall agricultural production was not deeply affected.

When our son was born, a nurse visited us at home to help the first-time parents get through the first days – a simple measure that can prevent untold expenses for later illnesses. Each neighbourhood has preventive health centres, separate from the clinics for the ill. This allows the early detection of a wide range of problems, and avoids the passing on of contagious diseases. To avoid excessive urbanization, cultural and scientific centres were distributed widely in small cities and towns throughout the country, in what was called the 'deruralization of the countryside'. This reduced the rural exodus, and ensured a more balanced population distribution, avoiding the dramatic demographic imbalances we find in developing countries.

On the other hand, the bureaucratic lid on the creation of small-scale initiatives would deprive the state corporations of the necessary support of countless diversified economic activities that are essential to the whole economic process whether the adopted system is socialist or capitalist.

It gradually became clear to me that there were many functional alternatives both to centralized bureaucracy and to savage liberalism: the point was to think about the institutional conditions required to support them. I also noted how the technocratic power of managers of state-owned corporations could be as broad as the technocratic power in private corporations: perhaps the ownership of the means of production wasn't the essential element after all.

Just as important was following the debate around constitutional changes, which in 1973 allowed the amalgamation of a large number of municipalities into larger ones. At first view a secondary and administrative matter, the measure in fact radically decentralized politics and changed the relations of power. Where previously a micro-municipality (*gmina*) had to appeal to the corresponding ministry for any purchase of an ambulance or hiring of police, now municipalities could resolve their problems locally. Thus decisions that had once been vertical and bureaucratized could now be resolved with greater participation of the interested citizens, and in an integrated manner, with more flexibility and efficiency. Thus political power spread horizontally, which would later open considerable space for the democratization movement.

On the theoretical plane, I came to understand that Marx pointed to socialization of the means of production as a way to transform political relations, to allow a society without class divisions. Thus transforming the relations of production (infrastructure) would allow a political (superstructure) transformation, creating a democratic society and a less oppressive state, making it impossible to maintain the domination of one class over another. The *actually existing* socialist societies, starting with the Soviet Union, had brought about the economic transformations, but not the corresponding political transformations. The soviets (which in Russian means 'councils') never got off the drawing boards. To socialize the economy without democratizing politics defeats the purpose. It would generate a system of state capitalism, changing how one reaches positions of privilege, but not the system of privilege itself.

At any rate, it was clear that the problem wasn't about the alternatives of communism/capitalism, privatization/nationalization, or lean state/welfare state, but rather the search for ways of ensuring economic dynamism with social balance. In reality, no regime has responded adequately to this prosaic yet immense challenge, which continues to dominate this dawning millennium.

Heading South

With the defeat of fascism in Portugal in 1974, the country was looking for professors to reformulate the teaching of economics, which was seriously outdated. I accepted an invitation from the University of Coimbra. Along with development economics, I would teach public finance in the Law Faculty. The last full professor had been a certain Professor Francisco Salazar. I succeeded him as best I could. The area of law still had an impressive level of formality. I presented a series of books to the assistant designated to me, and suggested that he read them, so that we could then discuss them. 'Discuss, Doctor? I came to listen to you'. The stern doctoral candidate looked at me, pleased as if he had laid an egg. Our uncertain pursuit of success leads us down some strange paths. It brought to mind some valuable advice of my father's: 'Never lose your sense of the ridiculous, the capacity to laugh at yourself.'

We are on a planet where the basic resources are being destroyed, where 11 million children die every year from ridiculous causes, where three billion people survive on less than two dollars per day, where around 50 armed conflicts are going on, and where a cultivated person who has had the privilege of a good education, and law on top of that, has nothing better to do than feed his own sense of self-importance.

I am not throwing the first stone. We are all vulnerable to attacks of pomposity. But we have an obligation to keep our perspective and sense of realism. It's not easy, when every television advertisement, every billboard, all the messages that bombard us daily offer us images of success, of superiority, of conceit. Years later, a student whom I had asked for his opinion in class, looked around at his colleagues and responded 'We at Esso think that...'. He had obviously just got a job. But did he need to borrow the authority of a multinational corporation – one, in fact, that has little to brag about in terms of moral standing? Isn't it enough for a person to claim the respect due simply to a human being? We'll come back to this, because this loss of personal identity is an epidemic spreading all over the planet, in proportion to the dominance and omnipresence of the means of communication.

I made two great friends, both economic ministers in the new Portuguese government, Mario Murteira and Francisco Pereira de Moura. With the extensive discussions about the process of nationalization and the pursuit of management alternatives, I was convinced that the time for simple solutions had passed. We had seen this at the end of the Allende government: what good does it do to socialize corporate ownership, if you still have to obey the logic of international links? A nationalized company in Chile needs to maintain its supply contracts with the United States, for example, or its Asian markets. A corporation is no longer an independent unit, but a link in the chain. Whoever is inside the system follows the rules. And the rules are very strict, as recognized by so many progressive governments who ended up implementing conservative policies.

Within a little more than a year, Portugal's future was sealed. The main option was to join the European Union (then the Common Market), and this option would determine the rest. The poor cousin would obviously not be dictating the rules. The Portuguese joked that they would have houses of the *maison* type, with *fenêtre*-style windows. Mario Soares was elected, a man with enough credibility on the left to implement a centre-right programme. He was roundly criticized from the left, but the essential elements were dictated by foreign relations, and any other leader would probably have followed the same path. Even at this time, it was clear that the form of integration into the global economy had become more important than domestic policy choices. And the range of internal options, of a country choosing its own path, had become increasingly narrow.

In Algeria we had all been refugees, guerrillas from different parts of the world. With the end of Portuguese colonialism, the friends from the time in Algeria were now ministers and ambassadors. A friend and politically dependable person, with a doctorate in planning and statistics, was welcome in the newly independent countries. I visited the Minister of Planning for Angola, in Luanda, but ended up accepting the invitation of Vasco Cabral, from Guinea-Bissau. I asked how much I would make, because as refugees we always had our hand out. He said I would earn more than he did, which was a way of saying it would not be very much. But I accepted gladly. I would spend four years in Africa, discovering other cultures, other values, and a wealth of human relations that I had never known existed.

In Luanda, even after a short visit, I had a very clear sense of the limitations of centralized government. All the senior government officials were in a constant frenzy to resolve problems, through virtually continuous meetings. But they met only with each other. Most of the population were left adrift, waiting for something to happen. Since they were not asked to participate in management, they never felt they had responsibility for anything. It was surprising how a government with unquestionably positive intentions could spin its wheels while sinking into increasing isolation, because of a lack of decentralized structures of public administration, and of organized participation by civil society.

It's not a question of who's to blame. Decolonization coincided with the peak of the Cold War. The process of independence had gained legitimacy, but any hint of social reforms would be immediately denounced as communism. Thus the African governments came to power without any chance of carrying out the reforms that would legitimate them in the eyes of the population. To respond to the immense demands for education, health, employment and income redistribution, they would have to mobilize the population, develop a state apparatus, and place restrictions on the colonial interests that remained active – and all these courses of action were seen in the West as evidence of Moscow's influence. Those that presented proposals for effective decolonization, with real social change, were systematically assassinated. Angola and Mozambique, as if the immense misery left from colonialism wasn't enough, had to confront the wars and sabotage that the West threw at them through South Africa. A huge opportunity to undertake social reforms, which could have emerged with the mobilizing impetus of independence, thus went down the drain. Africa, which had so little to do with the Cold War, would be one of its first victims.

Guinea-Bissau opted for a moderate path. I became the technical coordinator of the Ministry of Planning. Vasco Cabral, then Minister of Planning and later Vice-President, gave me his full support, with which I wasn't very sure what to do. I was suddenly obliged to forget all the macroeconomic models I had learned over the years, and look for ideas that could work. When the World Bank came with proposals for educational policy, I recommended rejecting them, because it would be better to concentrate this kind of investment in infrastructure, and maintain more freedom in the educational area. The Minister said he had no problem with this, but that I would have to prepare a convincing justification, because this would mean fewer schools for the children. I, with ideology in one hand, and technical models in the other, found myself poorly prepared for the actually existing economy. Only a small part of managing the economy actually has to do with economic models.

They were four passionate years, and everything that went well – the sight of something concrete actually working – brought immense satisfaction. I coordinated the technical preparation of the first national development plan, learning to combine credit systems with regional policies, to coordinate sectoral policies, to take into account political resistances, personal interests and vanities – a wide range of considerations without which no proposal survives, no matter how solid in technical terms. The economy is the lifeblood of a society, and everything has an influence on it. There is no mathematics that can replace good sense; a broad and multifaceted education; the capacity to understand, to listen, and to learn continuously; and, especially, the capacity of enjoyment, of taking a genuine interest in the matters at hand.

I spoke several languages, had a good technical doctorate, good political relationships, even if only on the left, and had no fear of working in poverty-stricken regions. Abdulrahim Farah, then the Under-Secretary-General of the UN, whom I had helped prepare some reports for Kurt Waldheim, invited me to New York to assume the post of economist in the Secretary-General's office, replacing the British economist James Ilett, who was retiring. But Vasco asked me to stay in Bissau, and I stayed. I could possibly have become a good high-level bureaucrat, but it would certainly have sterilized my taste for my work. We reached a compromise, with Vasco putting me in charge of the UN's planning programme in Bissau. I continued doing the same thing, but with an international status and salary. When visiting Farah in New York, at the United Nations headquarters, he introduced me to friends as the person who 'refused to come work with us because he had a commitment in Bissau'. The respectful smiles left it clear that they considered me a curious character, but Farah, an African, understood and showed genuine respect.

The salary was also a curious thing. My functions were unchanged, I still had the same diplomas, but my salary increased by a factor of ten. Before, I was paid as a national staff member; now I was an international 'expert'. They call this the labour market. In fact, there are parallel salary subsystems, supported by strong arrangements to protect the interests of particular groups. The labour *market*, I had come to discover, is a fiction. What market logic determines that teachers in Brazil earn less than one hundred dollars a month, while a corporate CEO earns over a hundred million? It is a question of political strength, not of economic mechanism. It sounds nice to speak of the labour market, because it implies that you are getting what you deserve. You are *free* to struggle for a better deal, and if you don't get it, blame yourself, not the system. And the market, obviously, does *not* correct the inequalities. The market has great respect for sheer power.

At the end of four years I had lost a good part of my liver to hepatitis, much of my hearing to chloroquine to fight malaria attacks, and various friends to the *coup d'état*. I considered that I had done my part and accepted another post in New York, as an adviser in the area of special political problems, which in reality dealt with critically impoverished countries. It was 1980, and Reagan, who had just taken office, had nominated an obsessive personality of narrow culture, Jeane Kirkpatrick, as US Ambassador to the United Nations. I landed at John F. Kennedy Airport, with a UN passport, a US visa and a formal invitation from Kurt Waldheim to assume my position. They didn't let me enter. I stayed three days in a little-known area of the airport, an immense room reserved for undecided cases. They refused to let me talk with the UN or return to Portugal, from where I had come. Brazil's then ambassador to the UN, who is now facing money-laundering charges, had given a thick file to Jeane Kirkpatrick, saying in no uncertain terms that I was a murderer and that my university degrees were forged, along with the rest of the stories assembled in the reports of Brazil's National Intelligence Service (SNI).

After three days they allowed me to return to Europe. When leaving I was able to see Fátima, who had already moved to New York because of my new position, and who had just given birth to our second son, André, at the Yale University hospital. We managed to exchange a few words, and I passed her a plastic bag, between two guards, containing my part of Kurt Waldheim's report to the General Assembly for that year, which she delivered to the Under-Secretary-General the following day. Days later, in Europe, I spoke by telephone with Gordon Goundrey, a Canadian and Deputy-Secretary-General, who explained that they didn't understand what was going on, but Kirkpatrick was threatening everyone, saying they would cut off funding, and that the United Nations was a nest of subversives. They were very sorry, but ....

I followed the advice of Paulo Freire, who suggested it was time for me to return to Brazil, where a general amnesty had been proclaimed. Fátima left from New York, and I from Europe, and we went to live in São Paulo, in Paulo's apartment near the Catholic University (PUC). I launched an administrative process against the United Nations and, after establishing that the accusations were false, they reinstated me. Gordon Goundrey informed me by phone that the informal condition was that I not ask for any position in the UN that required entering the United States, because this would mean applying for a visa, with all the problems that would imply.

It is important to recognize the scale of the problem: when the United States, after the Second World War, requested that the headquarters of the United Nations be located in New York, they committed themselves to respecting the right of the UN to receive whoever they wished. But, in practice, they obliged any employee of the United Nations to submit to the same conditions as anyone else applying to enter the United States, even a Minister coming to attend a meeting of the UN General Assembly. Such are the power relations at work, and the United Nations accepts them, even though legally the 'headquarters agreement' of its Charter ensures it autonomy. Might indeed does make right.

The ethical problem is just as important. Jeane Kirkpatrick acted on the information provided by the Brazilian Intelligence Service, but also based on the report of a CIA agent posing as a USAID official in Africa. When persons working for USAID, UNESCO or any other development or aid agency conduct work for the intelligence services or the US military, they are discrediting thousands of people throughout the world carrying out important work, who now come under suspicion. Today there is no doubt in my mind that the United States knew of the Nazi past of Kurt Waldheim, which gave them control over him. This could seem clever. But the practical effect is to build international relations based on cynicism, and to wipe out the patient work of building international solidarity that so many social actors carry out.

As for me, I thought I had learned all I could working for an international organization, so I thanked them for the offer and went to work for the Catholic University in São Paulo. The kaleidoscope turned again.

Back Home

I think coming home is never easy for anyone. Of course, there were the flowers and the welcome parties, but one does not live on flowers. We needed to reconstruct our existence, step by step, in the midst of a culture to which we had become strangers. I looked at the immensity of São Paulo, and thought of the immensity of what I had to learn again. The new generation of Brazilian economists didn't know me, and I didn't know them. The Ministry of Education, on the recommendation of the SNI, would take seven years to authorize the state university of São Paulo to recognize my degrees. In formal terms, I would continue to have only a high school education, even though I held several university degrees. No one recognized Fátima's years of study at the Piaget institute in Geneva, at the University of Warsaw and in Coimbra: she had to start in the first year, although they did waive the entrance examination. Amnesty was a narrow door, and power had not changed so much.

The Catholic University received me well. The anthropologist Carmen Junqueira helped me to make my way. Paul Singer wrote a positive evaluation of my dissertation, Joel Martins was enthusiastic about my participation in the graduate programme, and I was approved as a professor without waiting for any Ministry's decision. With some concern, I looked at my few remaining theoretical certainties, and asked myself what I would teach. I entered the graduate programme in administration, and shortly thereafter the Department of Economics. I discovered a striking complementarity between the knowledge of the international situation that I had acquired and the desperate lack of this kind of information among the students, a result of the barriers imposed by Brazil's military dictatorship. This situation, curiously enough, continues to the present day: even at the height of globalization, Brazil doesn't have a single media agency presenting dependable international information.

I divided my courses into presentations by my students and my own presentations. I taught the use of international reports, comparative economic development, and the economic system of multinational corporations. My students taught me that in Brazil 'you were either part of the steamroller, or part of the road'; that in the capital markets 'you were either on the inside making lots of money, or outside and losing it'; and that 'in Brazil selling on credit is very simple: the consumer doesn't understand anything about financial mathematics', and so on. For the second time, Brazil reabsorbed and digested me through its wealth of culture, humour, irony and despair. In Switzerland, you struggle to fit in: in Brazil, you struggle to avoid being swallowed up.

Someone who helped me right at the start was Caio Graco, from the publisher Brasiliense. I had gotten along well with his father, Caio Prado Júnior, in Paris. The dictatorship was, strangely enough, very good at creating friendships. Caio published my book about the economic history of Brazil, *Formação do Capitalismo Dependente no Brasil*, already published in several other countries, and then a theoretical book that I had written in Portugal and which Samir Amin used in his courses: *Introdução teórica à crise: salários e lucros na divisão internacional de trabalho*.

Marx's approach to the capitalism of his time had taken the nation as the unit of analysis, and specifically England. For developing countries, this perspective distorts the analysis, because the predominant influences on the formation of economic structures and on relations of production were external. In a sense, dominated as they were by developed economies, the poor economies were globalized ahead of their time. To analyse these economies by first analysing the reproduction of capital at the level of the *nation*, and later adding on international trade, would be a theoretical error. My approach was thus to use various ways of presenting models of reproduction of capital, to recalculate how the equations would look if international trade were included in the models themselves. The logic was clear: Brazil, for example, could maintain slavery right to the end of the nineteenth century and keep its workers in extreme misery – they needed them as producers, not as consumers, since the trade cycle relied on exchange with British producers. What we imported in exchange for our exports were luxury consumer goods and product-ion inputs, both for consumption by the dominant class, and thus did not require a capacity for mass consumption. These factors favoured a system which was very productive and which had a high concentration of income.

It was therefore not necessary to invent some colonial mode of production or other to explain what was simply a different subsystem of capitalist accumulation, whose logic was not limited to the national level, but based on its complementary role in the dominant system. It was the mechanism of reproduction of capital that sustained what would come to be called dependency theory. This analysis was a con-tinuation of my doctoral dissertation, allowing me to extend into the theoretical field of the internationalization of capital, essential for understanding the unfolding process of globalization, and the grow-ing distance both between rich and poor countries, and between the rich and poor in the poor countries. Even today, at the beginning of the millennium, Brazilian workers account for roughly one third of national income, compared with two thirds or more in developed countries.

The book I prepared outlining these ideas did not find a very enthusiastic reception. Caio Graco, in response to this relatively complex work, said that if I couldn't manage to say what I had to say in 50 pages, I had better forget it. He was then launching the very suc-cessful collection of small books, Primeiros Passos *(First Steps)*. I accepted the challenge, and set to work translating into Portuguese what I had written first in 'economese'. I discovered that there was no great mystery. To say that Brazil has a GINI coefficient of 0.63, something which no one understood except for half a dozen specialists, could be stated simply as: the 10 per cent richest families in the country account for 50 per cent of the income, which makes Brazil the most unjust country in the world, according to the World Bank, which is not known for its subversive tendencies.

Economic analysis does not need to be complicated. Or rather, it has to be complicated when one is trying to justify the unjustifiable – hiding reality. In a country where 1 per cent of the landowners hold half the agricultural land, and cultivate on average less than 5 per cent of their property, great theories are not required to show that the cause of so much hunger in the midst of such ample natural resources is simply the great fortune of land speculators. I wrote *Formação do Terceiro Mundo*, which was included in Brasiliense's collection *Tudo é História*, and it became a widely read book in Brazil. I discovered that it wasn't enough to do research: one had to communicate, and learn how to communicate. Recently a student at PUC told me that he liked what I wrote. I wanted to know why, expecting some theoretical comment. He said simply: 'It's that I understand it ....'

I also tried to present some of the realities that rarely enter works in economics, in the short study *Guiné-bissau: a Busca da Independência Econômica*. At one point, for example, the Dutch company HVA had the equipment of a large sugar production plant for sale. They sent a technical team to Bissau, which quickly produced three thick volumes showing that the country needed a sugar plant of exactly this size, even though it was absurdly oversized. They informed the Minister of Agriculture that HVA had sufficient influence in the Dutch government to obtain financing for the plant in the form of international aid, if the government formally requested the plant from them. With the request in hand, HVA would then pressure 'friendly' members of the Dutch government, using time-honoured mechanisms, and Holland would end up providing aid of x millions to Guinea-Bissau – not to

---

meet the country's most pressing needs, of course, but to buy the Dutch equipment. This is called 'tied aid'. Guinea gets a white elephant whose chronic deficits will be a permanent drag on the public accounts. The money never leaves Holland because it is simply transferred to HVA. HVA keeps the profit from the operation. The Dutch government gets votes by publicizing its generous help to poor countries. Dutch taxpayers foot the bill, along with the people of Guinea, who will have to support yet another ill-considered 'development' project. And the company, of course, will continue to sing the praises of market mechanisms, and say that all the ills come from the state.

Guinea-Bissau could refuse. But it is difficult to refuse a present that will create jobs, especially when domestic groups claim, out of their own interest, that it is a valuable project. Can one present cost-benefit calculations in a public demonstration? In this case, the operation was suspended because the Dutch Ministry of Foreign Affairs ordered an investigation and, supported by Vasco Cabral, aborted the operation. But dozens of other such operations worked, some with Brazilian intermediaries, producing economic disruptions. As happens with other poor countries, Guinea-Bissau could buy what the rich countries were willing to finance, and not what the country needed. Dependency generates dependency, and poverty generates more poverty.

Nicaragua, Nicaraguita

In 1986, the Nicaraguan government invited me to take over a United Nations project, similar to the one I had directed in Guinea-Bissau, but broader, supporting the creation of mechanisms for economic planning and regulation. Thus I returned to the United Nations, but in a more favourable context. I packed my bags yet again. Along with Alexandre who was already a teenager, André, Bruno and Sofia also went. Except for Alexandre, who had browner hair, they were all hopelessly blond.

Whoever has visited Nicaragua knows that it is a cultural shock. A happy, courageous, daring, disorderly, surrealist people – there is no strong adjective that doesn't apply. While I was waiting for a lost suitcase at the airport, a boy asked me about Brazil, full of curiosity. Everything I said amazed him: '*Alla…*!' he would exclaim. It was a few days before I understood that this was not a religious expression, but an abbreviation of the favourite comment of the Nicaraguans about anything surprising: '*A la gran puta…*!'

The Secretary of Planning and Budget was linked to the Presidency, and I focused on what a planning adviser can do most usefully: organize information and train staff. Both activities had permanent impacts, through improving decision-making capacity of local staff. I had to immerse myself in information technology, which had not been part of my background. It is a strange feeling to feel illiterate when one is nearing the age of 50. I was amazed by the potential of the new tools, which to an economist are what a Ferrari would be for anyone else. The revolutionary potential of being able to work with, store, organize and compare any information in a wide variety of ways and almost instantaneously was already clear, even in the early days of the XT personal computer. I became more aware that a phenomenal acceleration of history was under way, and that a knowledge society was gradually emerging.

Those two years were both both useful and pointless. We would take great pride in the electrification of an isolated region, only to see the installations destroyed the next day by the Contras operating from Honduras, equipped with the latest military technologies. Dressed like Martians, receiving details about each target from high altitude US observation planes, and protected in their camps on the other side of the border, they were difficult to combat. Their bases were veritable military supermarkets, with all manner of resources – from arms to bordellos, leisure, and of course salaries – later shown to be financed with drug trafficking, as in Vietnam. The world's mightiest democracy, of course, had to be right. Technological advances, in the absence of a correspondingly advanced civilization, mean only a capacity to reproduce tragedies more efficiently, and to carry out barbarities on a larger scale.

I received a visit from a group of US humanitarians, who were upset that, in the midst of immense deprivation and misery, the Nicaraguan government was refusing their medical assistance. The Americans are truly fantastic. They bomb, kill and injure, and then send bandages and medicines. And *they* are irritated when the injured don't appreciate their gestures.

In fact, it was a game of shadow boxing, the kind of puppetry displayed to such effect in the film *Farewell My Concubine*. In formal terms the Americans weren't involved, and they said that the Nicaraguan government should complain to the Contras, largely made up of Somoza's old hired killers. The government responded that they didn't want to talk to the clowns, but to the owner of the circus, in this case the American government. No one talked. Against this backdrop, economic development efforts fell by the wayside, because the country's limited but painstakingly accumulated wealth was wasted on the military effort. And an economy is absolutely indefensible when a few thousand professional soldiers armed with the most modern explosives and communication technologies can destroy whatever they want whenever they want, and take refuge on the other side of the border. And if the army followed them, there would be an international scandal: the Nicaraguans would be invading another country, a proof of their aggressive intent.

There were successful alternatives, such as the system of completely decentralized and highly participatory development that was implemented in the region of Estelí. The National Development Bank, rather than making decisions about credit in the distant bureaucracies in the capital city, created municipal credit councils, where large and small property owners and a range of social actors decided on the allocation of resources. If a farmer received money to purchase cattle and instead used it to speculate on the exchange rate, in the next meeting someone would ask: 'Where are the cattle – I didn't see them in your field?' Direct knowledge of the local situation is a powerful force for creating simple and flexible management, but demands that decisions be taken close to the interested populations, at the local level of administration.

It is not enough to analyse what decisions are technically most appropriate. Increasingly, one needs to define *who* makes the decisions. This insight brings political economy full circle, back to *institutional economics*, which had its heyday in the 1950s and was then abandoned for a simplistic 'anything goes' vision of business. Later, on a visit to China, I observed how a relatively broad public sector could be managed in a very decentralized manner by municipalities, permitting direct citizen control and a marriage of public interest with flexible and efficient management, in contrast to the centralized and bureaucratic system of the old Soviet Union.

In general, the Sandinista leadership believed they were the rightful owners of the reins of power, and could do what they felt was good for the people in a top-down manner. But there were some leaders who worked towards an effective democratization. To give a negative example, Jaime Wheelock, in agriculture, believed that agriculture only existed on a thousand hectares or more, and that the peasants just had to obey their leaders. In fact, there was no political space even to define a coherent development strategy. The constant pressure of the war reinforced the centralization of decision making, while disrupting the system. This, in turn, allowed its enemies to state that the government was incompetent. In two years of peace, soon after taking power, the Sandinistas had reduced illiteracy from 60 to 20 per cent. All this was to be lost, and the future was to be determined by the Cold War and by international interests, not by the prosaic needs of the population.

The issue of the political and institutional preconditions of economic development became central to my concerns. The neighbouring market economies, for example, such as Honduras and Guatemala, were and continue to be in chaos. In Nicaragua the state administered beauty salons, because they had belonged to Somoza, whose property was nationalized. Is a system more socialist because beauty salons are in the hands of the state? I had become aware that ideological simplifications didn't work, and that the subsystems that make up the economy were too highly differentiated to be able to apply undifferentiated linear policies, whether liberal or statist. The time is past when society was divided into proletariat, peasants and bourgeoisie, when the problems were of a national scope, and all could be reduced to the class struggle. Other models were needed.

Before leaving Managua I visited a personal friend, the late Henry Meyer, a highly cultured and humanistic Dutchman who was the United Nations representative in Nicaragua. While we talked, I leafed through one of these beautiful American tourism books, full of photos of lakes and mountains. I showed him a full-page photo with small white-sailed boats in the middle of a lake, with children peacefully riding bicycles on the shore, and the obligatory chapel in the background. We in Nicaragua dealt every day with the dead, the sick, the political crises. We both had the same observation, because of the contrast: how can people living in this environment in the United States possibly understand, or imagine, what underdevelopment is like, the reality of the Rocinha *favela* in Rio de Janeiro, or Heliópolis in São Paulo, or the violence in Guatemala that lies behind the innocent-looking bananas they buy in their supermarkets?

Generations

I went to visit my father, in the state of Maranhão, in the eastern Amazon. In 1964, while I was fighting with the embassies in Israel, he was growing tired of the Darwinian values in the hierarchies of the business world, publicly told a company president to go to hell, bought a boat with the severance cheque, and spent two years roaming along the rivers of the Amazon. At the age of 64 he discovered a new world. He bought a small house on the bank of the Tocantins river, in a village with 30 houses and no electricity, phone or bosses, and accessible only by water. The house cost 450 dollars. It was another planet. He discovered that people would die from anything there, so he called on his old friends in Europe, and received medicines, obtained an authorization to practice medicine, and started treating his neighbours. In a short time he had more than a thousand families registered as patients. He was, after all, an engineer. People stopped dying for no good reason. Every six months the children would get worm medicine. They all have worms, he said, we don't need a laboratory to tell.

Increasingly enthusiastic, he gave support to companies interested in investing in the region. Within a short time the troops arrived to disarm the peasants, and take away their shotguns and machetes. The peasants already knew that soon they would come to evict them. A neighbour killed a sergeant, then left the village and was never seen again. The soldiers returned, took his daughter, abused and killed her.

The important thing was to show who was in charge. For years my father tried to convince her mother to report the crime, but she would just say that she couldn't put her other children at risk. My father bought material, mapped the region, surveyed the squatters' land holdings, and they went *en masse* to the land registry office to obtain their title. He had become a guru, albeit a guru of the middle of nowhere.

One night I was invited to a local community meeting. A wizened old nun explained the Bible. One of the few residents who were not illiterate read where Joseph, in Egypt, proved himself a good manager: when the peasants lost their crops, and asked for grain from Pharaoh, Joseph opened up the granaries, but in exchange for the peasants' cattle; in the second year of poor harvests, he did the same in exchange for their land, and in the third in exchange for the peasants themselves. I am no doubt wrong about the order or the nature of the exchanges, but what is important is that the peasants lost everything, the Pharaoh got very rich, and Joseph became a great politician. In her soft voice, the nun explained that the Bible was a mirror, and that in this mirror of the past we had to learn to read the present. The peasants from the village began, one by one, to talk about how they had been pushed off their land, and how ranchers had burned their crops. The next day, drifting down the Tocantins river in the silence and tranquillity of the early morning hours – my time was up and I needed to return to São Paulo – I started thinking: this won't make the papers, but thousands of people in the country are doing this work at the grassroots, teaching human rights and dignity, building a foundation of consciousness so that tomorrow can bring deeper changes.

I was impressed with my father. First, because he had always held relatively conservative political positions, and had supported the military coup because he thought it would do away with corruption, the classic argument of dictators. Clearly, he had made a sharp about-face, and, living with the poor, he had discovered what the world looked like from below. I had already known something about this change, because he had written beautiful letters to my mother in

Poland, explaining his new understanding of things. I think it is striking that a man past 60 can profoundly rethink his values, and reconstruct his entire world view. This just goes to show how much our political positions, which may appear so obvious and rational to us, are influenced by how we are situated in the world.

I was also struck by the fact that he could, at his age, throw away all the comforts and privileges he was used to as an engineer, to rebuild his life from scratch – a new life that would last almost 30 years. Living in a city, he would have been another retired person seated in a waiting room. In Maranhão, he couldn't even spend his small pension, and he worked, helped others, and lived a full life. It was not 'I' and 'them' anymore, like it had been in Minas Gerais. He did things because they were useful, not to himself, but just useful. And for him it wasn't any sacrifice. He lived on the bank of a great river, fished whenever he wanted, and instead of noisy cars and irritated people going by his house, there were roseate spoonbills. I was more aware than ever of the idiocy of our desperate race to buy useless things, while we waste the only truly non-renewable resource: the time of our life.

He died at the age of 92 after living life to the fullest, even if without a refrigerator or television. In his last year of life he moved to the city of Imperatriz, because he was very weak. A good storyteller, he would sit on a bench in front of his house, and read the palms of young women to tell them their fortune. No woman can resist having their future told to them. And no man is serious, even at an advanced age.

My father passed away, as my mother had some years before in Poland. It took me almost fifty years to discover how deep our roots are. You don't need to be oriental nor believe in reincarnation to understand the force of continuity in our lives.

Local Power

I had barely left Nicaragua when I was invited by the new mayor of São Paulo, Luiza Erundina, to assume the post of Secretary in the municipal government, in charge of international relations, community organizations, and, curiously, the city police. The dominant impression was that of a gigantic bureaucratic machine, with more than 100,000 employees, mostly inherited from the period of the dictatorship, and devoted to managing privileges and corruption. The new mayor, Luiza Erundina, a woman of unquestionable dignity, honesty and fighting spirit, tried to turn the machine on its head, making it serve the city and, particularly, the sprawling and desperately poor *periferia*. No small challenge. For me these were four years of constant learning about how the dynamics of urban themes such as transport, garbage, water, housing, health and education are connected in a space like São Paulo.

São Paulo has 30 murders per day, a million people living in slums, and more than two million in overcrowded substandard housing. There is extensive pollution of the water bodies that one day will be indispensable to the city. Around 12,000 tons of solid waste per day are dumped in landfills, with no concern for groundwater contamination. There are around five million automobiles, in a city that grinds to a halt during rush hour because of an excess of means of transportation, itself a monument to capitalism. The subway, clearly the long-term solution for cities of this size, boasts a mere 45 kilometres of track.

And the land surface of this huge watershed – about 1,500 square kilometres – is two thirds impermeable, because no one thought to ensure sufficient soil permeability, as they do in other cities in the world. Sixteen million people passively observe the predictable floods every summer, many while sitting patiently in traffic jams, immobile, in cars that are designed, ironically, to go at more than 150 kilometres per hour. The largest economic centre in Latin America is managed by an eternal triad of construction companies, real estate speculators and corrupt politicians, in a multibillion dollar business that brings ample financing to the political campaigns that reproduce the system. And the political discourse is all about democracy and progress.

There was little awareness of the importance of international relations to a city. The International Relations department of Shanghai in 1992, when I went there to discuss strategies for large metropolitan areas, had around 140 staff members. The cities of Osaka and Toronto, to mention only a couple, have extensive international activities. And it's not just giving out the 'key to the city' or other ceremonial matters. It is in the direct relations between cities that the horizontal exchange systems are woven, with the gradual evolution from the world of vertical systems of authoritarian pyramids to a system of horizontal interactive networks. This process results from the new technologies that are revolutionizing communications, and the fact that the world is shifting from one of widely dispersed rural populations to one that is predominantly urban. Today any relatively large city has staff that travel to various parts of the world to see who is doing what to resolve problems such as pollution, criminality, transport and health care.

Cities face similar challenges, and they need to learn from each other, rather than reinventing the wheel. The profound ignorance about modern municipal policies results in thinking that transportation problems are resolved by building new tunnels and bridges for private automobiles, and that one reduces crime by buying more guns and police cruisers. In a sense, it is a matter of working through the implications for economic and social policies of the technological and demographic revolutions that are changing the planet. And in this process I am increasingly convinced that the municipality, and local authorities, have a fundamental role to play.

I now had a clearer vision of the strategic role of politics and institutions situated at the level where populations can have effective control over the processes. This, of course, is only a possibility, and does not simply happen. But the long years I have spent helping to create systems of economic planning and regulation in various countries have helped me to understand to what extent central government structures, in the absence of an 'anchor' in solidly organized local power that can press for results and demand a response to local needs, become dominated by a lurid carnival of pressure from developers, organized corruption schemes, designing bankers, subsidies to plants and other well-known pitfalls. Centralized governments can never find a balance by themselves; they need an external counterweight and control.

In other words, the concept of division of power between the executive, legislature and judiciary is not sufficient. We need the political ballast of organized civil society in local spaces, which is where, after all, the population lives and can check whether there is or is not real progress in terms of quality of life. In a mission I undertook to Costa Rica for the United Nations, I noted that municipalities there control only 5 per cent of all public resources. In contrast, in Sweden this figure is 72 per cent. In other words, Sweden doesn't have a smaller state, but rather its state operates primarily at the base, with direct control by the local population. And since the basic needs of the population, such as schools, family doctors, transport, bread and milk, or security, are basically local-level activities, it is simply a matter of putting the pyramid right side up, with the base of the population having a predominant weight in economic decisions. And the choices in public decentralized policy become much more democratic, efficient and flexible than the centralized decisions of huge private corporations.

The experience of progressive management in São Paulo helped me see much more clearly the enormous potential of decentralized forms of public administration. Such profound changes are not, of course, completed in four years and in one municipal administration term. Today in Brazil this process is moving forward steadily, especially in the state of Rio Grande do Sul, even though the traditional systems of corruption – contractors, pork-barrelling politicians, real estate speculators, the media and corrupt sections of the judiciary – largely persist.

The most promising options for local organization, in terms of achieving social equilibrium and efficient management, have generally emerged in left or centre-left administrations. This should come as no great surprise. The left, immersed in its traditional vision of overall state control, saw its world collapse, and is reconstructing much more advanced approaches than the right, which is still trapped in its corruption and backwardness, and continues to repeat a formula that is basically restricted to backing big business. The successes of progressive approaches have often compelled the right to unite to block the experiments. But this is part of the game. The crucial thing is that through the patient work of thousands of individuals, civil society organizations, and a growing number of businesspeople looking for new approaches, a new and profoundly transformative vision of social management is emerging. Today there are hundreds of experiences of this type under way in Brazil, even though centralization still often predominates.

The Era of Globalization

There is a growing perplexity in the world – though it is not shared in the dominant countries, and especially not in the large US-based corporations, where a great simplification of maximization of profit rules, and where ethics in international relations is often reduced to the attitude so common today, even if it is only expressed in private: 'We're the best, f... the rest.'

The rest, however, continues to exist. And today it is four fifths of the world's population. I was invited to work as a consultant in South Africa, which was gradually emerging from the long dark period to which it was subjected, not by 'backward and poorly trained' populations, but by rich and highly educated whites. This in itself is significant. We are so blinded by respect for technical competence, that we forget the principles that this competence should serve. This is the basis of the immense human stature of Nelson Mandela, in the face of the powerful and wealthy exploiters of gold and diamonds. No degree of competence can help if the wrong objectives are pursued.

Today South Africa is pursuing ways to recover its capacity to govern, in the face of two powerful forces of change: internally, the shift from apartheid to democracy; and, externally, the opening up and globalization of the economy. How to rebuild a consensus within a society when the so-called international financial community demands 'credibility and confidence'? It is not easy to tell the population to wait. With the white population (13 per cent) receiving 54 per cent of the family income, the situation is almost identical to Brazil's, where 10 per cent of the richest families take home 50 per cent of the income.

The dilemma is simple. The people demand minimal social and economic conditions, jobs, conditions for survival with a minimum of dignity. Transnational corporations, on the other hand, demand financial 'reliability' – in other words, respect for profits, concentration of incomes, and freedom to export capital. If they are not ensured all the privileges, they get upset and leave, throwing the country into an exchange crisis. And if they are given these privileges, they concentrate income, and deepen the political and social crisis. If our instruments of development, in this case large corporations, are pernicious if we don't give them what they want, and useless if we do, clearly we need to rethink their contribution to economic development. The simplistic vision of attracting capital to develop a country, or a region, is not well-founded. The source of dynamism should be internal, and aimed at the direct interests of the local population itself. And in this case the complementary contribution of corporations can be useful.

South Africa, with a *per capita* annual income of around US$3,000, is by far the richest country in the region. With 41 million inhabitants and a territory of 1.2 million square kilometres, it is a large country by any standards. Add 40 per cent of global reserves of gold, 88 per cent of platinum, and 83 per cent of manganese, chromium and vanadium, along with being between second and third place in the world for coal, diamonds, asbestos, nickel, titanium, uranium and zinc. The country produces 50 per cent of the electricity of the continent, and contains 45 per cent of the paved roads. The economic weight of the country is thus immense. Shouldn't this be of great advantage in international negotiations?

Protected for decades by apartheid itself, South Africa had built up a huge industrial infrastructure, similar to Brazil's, but with relatively low productivity, and based on very low wages. Today, forced to confront low-priced products from Asia, and the repayment of the social debt to a non-white population getting tired of waiting, and demanding wages and social benefits, South Africa has discovered that it is not enough just to have a modern industrial sector. The overall balance of the economy, and particularly the reduction of social exclusion, are essential. The problem is aggravated by rural dynamics, where only 12 per cent of the land is cultivated, and the large properties owned by whites have benefited from huge subsidies, without which their survival is threatened. You cannot expect 'market forces' to solve this kind of structural problem, you need planning and conscious intervention.

The country has avoided the magic model of privatization. According to the President's White Paper on reforming public services,

> the Government is well aware that in some countries [privatization] has had adverse effects, in terms of declining quality of services, worsening working conditions for employees, growing unemployment and marginalization of more fragile groups, especially women and children. The movement towards leaner and more cost-efficient public services in South Africa will thus be based not on privatization but on the creation of effective partnerships between government, labour, companies and civil society, and on the construction of a high degree of involvement of communities in local service provision.

But attempts are also made at creating more efficient systems of economic governance. The dynamic appears clearly in the operations of the National Economic Development and Labour Council (NEDLAC). The Council brings together the labour movement, corporations, the financial sector, and civil society organizations to discuss concrete solutions to the country's key problems. Once agreement is reached and formal commitments made on the part of key actors in the country's economic and social machine, the decisions are forwarded to Parliament to provide the corresponding legislation.

Rather than decisions being made through third parties, they are made directly with those affected, and the Members of Parliament, whose job it is to legislate, do just that. This approach is also adopted by governments of the nine provinces as well as the municipalities, with a philosophy of government that transcends the traditional privatization/

nationalization see-saw that drives discussions in other countries, pursuing instead flexible and participatory mechanisms through negotiations at the various levels of public administration. The approach taken by the government in fact enriches the fabric of control of civil society over the state and the economic arena, overcoming the absurd alternative offered to us of being controlled either by state monopolies or by private cartels.

What have we read about it? The important changes in South Africa, and the possible implications for other developing countries, simply do not appear in the news. South Africa is mentioned when there is trouble between Nelson and Winnie Mandela. That is what really counts.

Is the experience successful? In this area there are no guarantees, and the key point (including a comparative understanding of the dynamics from the perspective of Brazil), is to be aware of the extremely narrow room for manoeuvre that is left to developing countries, pressured internally by exploited and increasingly aware populations, and externally by the recommendations of the 'international financial community'. Venezuela is exploding because of popular pressure and the war waged by minorities to maintain their privileges. Mexico imploded a few years ago because of the dissatisfaction of the financial community, which withdrew its capital and left the country to its fate. Financial speculators pushed Argentina down the same path. Brazil managed to end inflation, which is a huge advance for the population that suffered most from its rampage. This respite has gained time, but both foreign and domestic debt are soaring, preparing new dramas. Other countries, such as most of sub-Saharan Africa, are completely adrift.

In other countries, one cannot separate religious fundamentalism from the fact that the model imposed on them, based on oil exports with obscene privileges for a few families, and poverty for the majority of the population, can only lead to despair. Making Saddam Hussein the bad guy and maintaining the Saudi and other ruling princes as good guys – not to mention making use of Israel for the dirty work –

can only be seen as a cynical policy. We really do have to think economics through again, in its deeper social and political implications, with the overall objective of improving the quality of life of the population.

We have entered the new millennium without a single serious support mechanism for development of the poor countries, and we are speaking of four fifths of the planet's population. There are clear signs of the tragedies on the way. The US presidency announces the importance of landing a manned mission on Mars in 2015. Meanwhile, we are unable to cope with the mosquito that transmits malaria, killing 2.5 million people every year. In the face of the real global challenges, the US is just absent, Europe is centred on its own organization, and global corporations – particularly in the financial sphere – have become uncontrolled giants that roam around the world picking off short-term opportunities.

Each country is a case. I was invited to comment on the transformations in the governmental structure of Mongolia. Getting there wasn't easy. From Brazil you go to Johannesburg, in South Africa, then take a one-day flight to Bangkok, Thailand, and so on to Hong Kong, in the south of China, and finally reach Beijing. The next plane flies over China, leaves the Great Wall behind, and after a few more hours the view from the airplane window is the immense plateau of the Gobi desert, a perfect horizon of clean air that we don't see in the West, the vast steppes dotted with the age-old traditional tents of Mongolia.

The images that come to mind are inevitably those of Genghis Khan and the fearsome horsemen who conquered one of the greatest empires the world has ever known. As the plane descended, we could see more clearly the herds of sheep, the horses and the wide, shallow river valleys. One got the impression of a past that had changed little, an impression soon confirmed by the ancient temples overlooking the old capital, Ulan Bator.

How is it that this pristine space has survived, this immensity of fields without fences or trespassing signs, lost among the endless steppes of Siberia? How is it that a nation of little more than 2.5

million inhabitants has survived, along with their language, their culture, their unique customs, while wedged between two military, economic and cultural heavyweights like Russia and China?

Mongolia wanted to decentralize its management system, as part of an approach based on opening up the country and applying market mechanisms. I was struck by a sense of surrealism: the Western formula has reached even here; the simplification that transforms human ideals into an all-purpose recipe. What will the outcome be of the marriage of this isolated region and its traditions, with the speculative systems of the global financial casino?

Ulan Bator reflects all this surrealism. Prior to the arrival of Western simplifications, the capital was subject to Soviet simplifications. The huge squares in the centre are bounded by gigantic buildings, replicas of the buildings of the Russian bureaucracy – a heavy, grey style that contrasts sharply with the beautiful architecture of the traditional temples, with their refined colours and delicate form. Just beyond are the new buildings symbolizing the arrival of the global era in Mongolia: the soaring towers of Western hotel chains, dozens of storeys tall, just as oppressive, although in a different style, as the bureaucratic buildings. The conclusion appeared obvious: the arrogance of Russian communism and of global capitalism is identical – each imposes its stamp, neither thinks of adapting to traditions, respecting cultures, or even just fitting into the striking natural beauty of the country.

Within the hotels were the busy multinational locusts, with their neat haircuts and black briefcases, seeking the profits of this new frontier. Mongolia is rich in gold, tungsten, zinc, molybdenum, silver, and high-value timber. To the local governments, bewildered by the pace of events and the corporate invasion, they explain that the liberty to market their products means that the country is free, and therefore democratic and modern. The Americans buy up the gold, the Koreans install modern telecommunication systems, and the Japanese offer luxury cars. Most of the population, living in modest apartments from another era, or in the tents that surround the city, are mere spectators.

Caught in a strange mixture of fear and fascination, like the majority of us today on the planet, they dutifully play out the roles assigned to them, without comprehending the spectacle going on in the country.

What sense is there in globalizing Mongolia? They will be served up with French fries to global speculative capital. The forests that line the crystalline rivers will be turned into toothpicks. They will appear in our supermarkets with the label 'Made in Mongolia'. The children will no longer face the cold in cavalcades on the steppes. They will be happy, sitting at home in front of a television, watching Starsky and Hutch. Or if Brazil is successful in its dealings with Turner and Murdoch, watching the latest Brazilian *telenovela*. And Mongol historians will recognize that dealing with China and Russia had been a piece of cake.

Canada is a completely different story. Of course they are influenced by the obsessive consumerism of their southern neighbours. When my mother visited Canada in the 1960s, she went to Mass in Toronto's Polish community. During Mass, the priest asked for all to pray for their poor compatriots suffering under the yoke of communism in Poland. Feisty as always, and actually living in Poland, my mother completed his sermon for him by explaining that she would ask her church in Warsaw to pray for the Canadian Poles, who lived life as if it were nothing but a visit to the supermarket.

But the fact is that Canada is maintaining its distinctive and fascinating character. Here, globalization encounters highly structured communities, and a national determination that the country won't be swallowed up. Resistance may appear to be centred on small things. Visiting a supermarket in Toronto, I came across a room full of books. They explained that it was a section of the municipal library, which operates within the supermarket. The logic is simple: when someone comes to do their shopping, they take out a book for the week, and return the one from the previous week. In microeconomic terms, in terms of revenue, of course the supermarket would prefer to have a section of beauty creams. But in terms of quality of life and civic involvement, having this ease of access to books, being able to look through them with the children, stimulating an interest in culture, clearly increases social productivity. It is obviously a question that involves priorities. If money is the reference, the priority has to go to beauty creams. But if we include time as a value, things change.

The key here is that it is not a matter of choosing between the supermarket and books, out of economic or social interest – it is a matter of integrating them. And in many countries, the integration of these interests has already been incorporated into society's current management practices, in concepts such as *partnerships, empowerment, governance, accountability*. The participatory budgeting already applied in many Brazilian cities allows precisely for this kind of integration between the immediate economic interests, and the broader social needs.

In São Paulo, the recycling programme was cancelled by a right-wing politician because it wasn't economically efficient. The reasoning is correct from a microeconomic perspective: recycling costs more than the return from selling the recycled product. In Canada, however, once the attitude or culture of eliminating waste became widespread, the amount of remaining organic waste produced was much lower, and could be collected once a week. In São Paulo, daily collection of 12,000 tons generates huge costs. This means a dramatic difference in costs for the city. Cultural change, the contribution of millions of daily small actions by every individual, such as separating clean waste, thus brings about a great improvement in social productivity.

There is no great secret to the process. A private company can carry out activities that create a marketable product, like shoes. When dealing with diffuse interests of society, however, such as clean rivers, the beauty of a city, green space for children to play in, school–community integration, the wealth of life in rivers and oceans, there is no company that can sell this to us, except by walling off a region and building gated communities, ghettoes of wealth that generate new crises in the future. In economic terms, this is counterproductive: it reduces the availability and supply of free goods by transforming them into marketable products. Whether the issue is water, ocean fish stocks, land or beaches, the mechanism is the same, reducing supply to increase the value. The result is that increasing profits demands a reduction of social wealth. Considering the growing demand for social consumption – clean rivers, security and the like – the narrow market approach becomes a growing problem.

A strong role for the public interest and for civil society is essential here. It's easy to say that this involves rich societies, where there is a culture and space for activities of this type. But we could reverse the logic. Canadian society is much less wealthy, in the narrow concept of GDP, than that of the United States, but the quality of life is much higher. Seen from another perspective, we could ask if Canada has managed to develop these kinds of initiatives because it is rich, or whether it became rich because it chose more socially productive routes. It is very telling to see the extent to which the culture of good economic and social sense, and what has been called 'social capital', generates a range of spin-offs in terms of economies and social productivity: schools open their sports facilities to the community at nights and on weekends, which increases the available infrastructure and leisure opportunities, with obvious impacts in terms of health, reduced drug abuse, and so on. The availability of leisure activities, clean rivers or swimming pools, for example, reduces the absurdity of rich families building individual swimming pools, which go unused almost all the time, with high costs and almost zero productivity.

Wouldn't it make sense to reproduce practices that have already proved themselves? What this means, for improving social management, is that social progress doesn't only mean allocating more resources to education. It also means incorporating into business, government, community or individual decisions the diverse dimensions and impacts that each action can have in terms of quality of life. Social policies, beyond being one area among others – which includes the obvious sectors of health, education, housing, leisure, culture, information, sports and the like – also constitute one facet of all other activities: a way to conduct industry, a manner of thinking about urban development, a way of using rivers, a form of organizing trade.

In Brazil, an interesting example is the agreement between a supermarket chain and the government of Rio Grande do Sul, under which the supermarket allocates part of its space to small retailers to avoid causing unemployment, and purchases some of its inventory directly from small rural producers. It is not corporate charity, but rather good sense in the integration of economic, environmental and social objectives. The company improves its reputation and good name, politicians gain visibility, and society gains jobs and economic activities. The only losers are certain ideologues, blinded by their obsession with pure models.

The microeconomic concept of productivity only manages to prove its superiority when it isolates the profit impact of a production unit from the set of externalities – the social and environmental impact. For each park that closes to make way for a supermarket or a parking lot, we have greater profit in business terms, and greater losses in economic terms, because of the additional costs generated to society, along with the losses to quality of life, which after all is the broader objective.

How do we feel in the midst of this process? Most of us just feel lost. If we have a hungry child at home, family or not, whatever the race or religion, we will feed it. As society grows complex and globalized, the causal chain between our individual or corporate behaviour, and the impact in some corner of the world, gets much longer, and this favours a gradual dilution of responsibility. What is the link between the struggle of a city in the United States trying to keep the jobs in a local arms-producing company and the African dramas? It all goes through a complex system of international arms trade, which makes the US responsible for almost 48 per cent of world sales. Isn't it easy to say that the Chinese would take over the trade if the US abandoned it? And that the person who is investing in these corporations is just trying to optimize the gains on legitimately earned savings. The practical result is lethal high-technology weapons in the hands of children or any group having diamonds to trade – a recent example – and nobody responsible for it. The longer the causality chain, the greater the responsibility gap. A hungry child in our house is a scandal. But 11 million dying every year of similar causes is 'unfortunate'.

How does this work in practice? In Brazil we calculated that when you buy a box of vitamin C, paying about 3 dollars, you are actually paying for 1.5 cents-worth of ascorbic acid. Of course, you are also paying for the 'natural' orange flavour, and the silver paper and other niceties, not to speak of the advertising that will convince you that your purchase is a bargain. In practice, at this price, two thirds of the Brazilian population are unable to purchase vitamin C. Since ascorbic acid is a powerful preventive medicine, society in general will have to pay for the extra health costs. The system works because the producers are big multinationals, organized – in the case of Brazil – in a cartel of 21 corporations, with heavy investment in advertising to generate brand respectability, generously paid for by the price we pay. Curiously, the corporate manager would feel very 'unethical' if he undersold his colleagues, allowing market forces to determine prices.

The option centred on immediate profit to the business unit is not only socially unjust; it is economically perverse. It is natural for a complex society, faced with fast-paced change, frightened by unemployment, and concerned about violence, to seek simple solutions. The great ideological simplification of liberalism in this sense represents the ideological mirror image of the former great simplifications of the state-centred left. Shrugging off these extremes inherited from the twentieth century, we have to learn to build more complex systems, where the key word is not the right choice between extreme models, but the integration of more diversified interests into a more balanced development.

Science, Conscience, Experience

These different moments of life experience all contribute to a more general picture, where ideas, values and feelings gradually build, like the parts of an oriental mosaic, a vision of the world. We all feel in ourselves this complex assortment of small parts, each little stone having its own value, and the different value of the overall image to which each stone contributes. There is no isolating one part from the others.

The loss of our capacity to view the whole picture, the fragmenting of the parts, is perhaps our most significant and tragic inheritance from the Anglo-Saxon world of values. David Korten, in his book *The Post-Corporate World*, neatly sums up this dilemma:

> When the modern corporation brings together the power of modern technology and the power of the great mass of capital, it also brings in the scientist whose self-perception of moral responsibility is limited to advancing objective instrumental knowledge, and the corporate executive whose self-perception of moral responsibility is limited to maximizing corporate profit. The result is a system in which power and expertise are delinked from moral accountability, instrumental and financial values override life values, and what is expedient and profitable takes precedence over what is nurturing and responsible.

A company is accorded a legal personality, as if it were in fact a person with desires and rights, but it is fixed on a single objective, that of making profits, because this denotes efficiency, competence and thus moral value. There is a magical appeal and unquestionably a good deal of charlatanism in this approach, which does not stand up to a vision of the whole. Once you artificially isolate techniques from ethics, no limit can be set on what the company does, as long as it obtains profits; nor any limit on what its employees do, since they are only following the company's orders. This delinking of economic activity and moral accountability permits, for example, a company to sell arms all over the planet with the justification that it merely produces good mechanisms that happen to fire projectiles. Similarly, a financial company may sack the accumulated savings of a country and explain that it was only defending the interests of its investors, thereby fulfilling its obligations.

Of course, if a client country is not sufficiently aware of its weapons necessities, there will be substantial bribes to convince it. And if the financial waters are too calm to allow opportunistic financial gambling, a small destabilization may liven things up, as Joseph Stiglitz has shown in detail. Corporate ethics adopts the profound philosophy of the 'wall' in a soccer free kick: the key is to avoid advancing alone, always to advance through little steps, and to stay in line with the others. This in turn allows the mother of all arguments: *everybody does it*. Ethics becomes diffuse and diluted in terms of what is socially acceptable, and acceptable because it is widespread in a particular social milieu. A person concerned with the quality of life, with solidarity, or with the environment will be presented as an idealist, as a dreamer who is out of touch with the 'real world'. In the same dominant media that promote this kind of message, we can see daily interviews with executives and politicians who look at us with an air of professional knowledge, selling us the idea that they know the *real* world.

To what point can we keep moving the wall forward? There is even a concept to define the limits: 'plausible deniability'. That is, the company can continue with its mischief as long as the denial of guilt remains plausible. It is enlightening to see the angelic expressions of the line of players, a few metres from the ball, looking at the referee like innocent maidens who don't understand why he should be so concerned. The difference with the economy, of course, is that it could involve a drug that is so overpriced that millions of people will not have access to it. No one is innocent – we are all responsible for what is happening.

In the first part of this book, I referred to experiences, suggesting that they were moulding a search for responses through scientific instruments; life experiences and science tend in turn to build our values, feelings of guilt or responsibility, of satisfaction or indignation. As professors, we are not only mathematicians, or geographers, or economists: we are human beings with all our richness and all our weaknesses. Building a wall around our technical capabilities, in order to be 'scientifically objective', is just plain rubbish. We have to look at the whole chain of practical results linked to our actions.

In the second part, we will attempt an even more risky task, that of trying to organize more systematically the world view that has emerged from this mixture of scientific work, moral indignation, and accumulated experience. Not that the directions are entirely clear. In this historical phase of profound transformations, the common denominator is probably the futility of predictions. However, it is worth examining the macro-trends that are emerging, and peering through the fog to identify the outlines of the new world we are building.

In the third part, we will come back to Pauline, to values, and to the new trends that give us hope.

PART 2
Mosaic of the Future

New Dynamics, Other Concepts

There are moments in which the innumerable facets of reality and the received theories really don't match. Never has there been such polarization between dominant and dependent countries, such an absurd financial or commercial manipulation, and yet we no longer feel comfortable with simply denouncing imperialism. The gap between rich and poor is widening, including within developed countries, but the traditional concept of class struggle seems to have become inappropriate. We still talk about capitalism and the bourgeoisie, but a growing number of studies, from UNCTAD reports to the work of more conservative research bodies, point to the fact that not only workers, but also productive businesses that bring real benefits to society, are being undermined through global financial speculation. In a certain way, traditional concepts have become outdated, they don't seem to reflect reality anymore. They no longer light our path adequately.

Thus, at the same time that the reasons for concern and a critical approach are growing stronger, our analytical instruments are proving less adequate. The solution is surely not to set the theories aside, but rather to rethink the concepts that should lead us to an understanding of the new trends. The task becomes more urgent in the light of so many social movements throughout the world organizing under new banners, which have less and less to do with the traditional state-centred vision of the left, and even less to do with the simplifications of the Washington consensus.

For me, making sense of the key changes under way was a useful point of departure. These changes, reflected in particular in the technological revolution, globalization, the global polarization between rich and poor, in the widespread urbanization of the planet, and in the transformation of work relations and organization, all pose new challenges.

Each of these trends carries its own embedded contradictions. Technologies are advancing rapidly while the corresponding institutions advance slowly, and this is an explosive mixture, because we are not finding the institutional solutions to manage the ample planetary impact of the new technologies. New technologies have generalized overfishing throughout the world, for example, leading to the destruction of life in the seas. Discussions on how to cope with the problem have been going on for decades, and while we discuss, life is disappearing.

The economy has become global in various aspects, while the systems of government remain under national jurisdictions, generating an international space with no rules and a general loss of governance. The behaviour of financial speculators, and the potential for fraud seen in the Enron affair (and so many others) is a good illustration of this case. In the international arena nowadays, it is becoming the law of the jungle. The planet has no central bank, and our savings are being played with in the global cassino, instead being used for productive investment and development.

The distance between rich and poor is increasing dramatically, while the planet shrinks and urbanization brings the extremes of society into proximity, leading to contradictory and increasingly unsustainable disparity and generating widespread violence and insecurity. A simple look at Rio de Janeiro, at the absurd mix of luxury and *favelas,* makes this evident. Visiting *favelas* has actually become an attraction for tourists.

Urbanization itself has shifted the space of management of our everyday life to the local sphere, while systems of government continue to follow the centralized logic of the first half of last century, when population was mostly rural and dispersed, so that government was in the capital city. With urbanization, most of the initiatives linked to the quality of our lives and environment depend on a strong participatory and decentralized management, while central government itself needs this kind of organized, city-based management to function adequately in its broader sphere.

Finally, the same system that places more advanced equipment in the hands of workers generates social exclusion, transforming the majority into passive spectators, increasingly fed up with the new technologies that generate new threats while hiding from sight the solutions to their most elementary problems. Huge networked corporations marketing their soft drinks, fast food, tennis shoes and other products (including services) oust local producers, offer few jobs, and generate a deeper economic and social divide.

The conclusions we can draw from these five contradictory processes is that we urgently need to bring some organization to this kind of chaotic growth and equip ourselves with the institutional means to capitalize on scientific advances that are positive in themselves but presently disruptive. Growth has to be guided towards sustainable development and improved quality of life. It certainly is a huge task, but we cannot go on pretending we are not seeing the approaching crises. The technological instruments humanity wields are just too powerful to allow us to wait for some 'invisible hand' to protect us.

There is widespread frustration with ideological 'Christmas trees', whether they promise social tranquillity through nationalization and planning, on the one hand, or, on the other, prosperity through privatization and the invisible hand. The first has led to a gigantic bureaucratic muddle, while the second is leading us to the most dramatic accumulation of social injustices that humanity has ever known, and a permanent sense of insecurity. This is not a matter of winners or losers. For now the loser is humanity itself. The key is to find forms of social management that allow us to address our problems effectively.

A cold look at the ways that we organize and govern ourselves should make us feel modest, at the very least. There aren't many reasons to celebrate, not in Brazil, nor in China, Russia or the United States, for that matter. I am convinced that today the best approach is not another simplifying certainty, but an open-minded approach of frank questioning, political creativity, tolerance and understanding. It is essential to keep the communication channels open between the various social sciences, between different types of institutions, and between the range of organized social players.

To say we are confused is at the same time true and not true. The paths open to us are undoubtedly more complex, but it is increasingly clear that the objective is a more humane society, with more solidarity, with less waste of our limited planetary natural resources. There is also a cultural change looming, as more people are getting tired of the absurd models of identity that lead women to pump themselves full of silicon, and men to pose as self-important executives. A touch of realism should give us some humility: we haven't even managed to reduce the number of children dying of hunger on the planet, or to ensure a decent family and community environment for our children, or even to feel secure in our homes.

Modesty is really not our forte. In addition, as individuals we have a strong propensity to convince ourselves that we have found the *diritta via*, the Straight Path, that others, whether through bad faith or ignorance, regrettably fail to recognize. It is good to feel we know the way. It allows us to look confidently to the future, to a path that ignores sacrifices. Such confidence is being undermined by profound transformations that leave us in a state of perplexity. Some, in the resulting insecurity, hold on more tightly to the eternal truths. Others shout the old slogans more loudly, in the hope that they will be better heard. But we can't escape from the need to rethink our course.[4]

The *diritta via* once consisted of economies that were national, centred on industrial production and directed by bourgeois champions

---

[4] Dante's hero was modest: 'Nell'mezzo del cammin di nostra vita, mi ritrovai per una selva oscura, che la diritta via era smarrita' ('Midway along the journey of our life I woke to find myself in a dark wood for I had wandered from the straight path') – Dante, *La Divina Comedia* (trans. Mark Musa).

who had exhausted their historic role and were preparing to cede leadership to the new industrial working class, ready for its part to assume the rudder through the socialization of the means of production. The transformation would come about through control of the state. To consider this version of the *diritta via* gives us the feeling that we have when looking at old, yellowing photos in a family album. An objective comparison with the world we live in gives us a sense of how much the parameters have changed. The national economy is being absorbed by the global economy, industry is giving way increasingly to other activities, and the bourgeoisie, in the traditional sense of owners of the means of production, are being replaced by rational and implacable technocrats, if not by speculators completely indifferent to the prosaic realities of producers and consumers. The working class has become extremely diversified in the context of the new social complexity, and its comprehension increasingly resists the traditional simplifications. Socialization of the means of production changed course, and the state is pursuing new functions in coordinating, and no longer replacing, social forces. The change, it must be emphasized, is qualitative, with all the implications this has for our theoretical frameworks.

Another *diritta via* consisted of the specialization of each nation in the search for comparative advantages, and in the free movement of microeconomic decisions, guided by simple personal interest. What's left of the comparative advantages when 3.5 billion inhabitants of low-income countries have a total GDP of about one trillion dollars, while a group of rich countries, with less than 15 per cent of the world's population, controls about 80 per cent of global GDP? Comparative economic advantages cannot exist if the players are not remotely comparable by the measure of political and economic power. And the relative advantages that some countries have are selectively absorbed by transnational corporations that distribute their production processes by locating their labour-intensive activities in Asian countries, where they pay a few cents per hour, their engineering-intensive factories in Russia, where advanced technical capacity can be bought for a few hundred dollars a month, and so on. For there to be comparative advantages for the nation, the economic spaces need to be constituted by nations, but this is only partly the case nowadays.

The microeconomic logic doesn't fare much better. The idea was that the baker would have every interest in producing good bread, cheaply, and in great quantities, because he would thus earn good money, and the baker's concern for his self-interest would result in ample bread for all. It currently results in a simplified version of the utilitarian perspective, which has become the dominant applied philosophy. The outlook of the baker and the belief in the automatic resolution of the macro tensions that result in millions of microeconomic decisions become ridiculous on a planet that faces the impact of giant transnational groups, the powerful networks of arms merchants, the global media monopolies, the rapid destruction of sea life, global warming, acid rain, global financial speculation, the illegal trade in drugs, human organs and child prostitutes, and so many other manifestations of an economic process over which we have lost control. Actually existing global capitalism is a new phenomenon, and the conceptual tools for analysing it are still in their infancy. To apply the old concepts of Smith or Ricardo, and believe in the magical power of something now so complex and differentiated that we smile when we call it 'the market', leads us back to those yellowing photographs.

It is not surprising that we find it difficult to rethink the social universe from a new perspective. First, because the changes occurred quickly in historical terms, vertiginously even, but also progressively, with no precise moment of rupture. As a result, we are in a sense stretching our concepts to cover an increasingly different reality. The 'lumpen proletariat' has taken on a broader meaning in the concept of 'social exclusion', while the 'proletariat' has evolved into the more general concept of 'workers', for example. To refer to the coordinated system of power of around 500 transnational companies, or the intra-company transactions at administered prices that today involves 35 per cent of global trade, as 'the market', has become unjustifiable, and the old concepts have been patched up with terms like 'managed market'. What is a market when instead of 'free' it has become 'managed'?

When a child grows, one can let out the seams of its clothes. But there comes a moment when it is necessary to look for another shirt.

We hold on to the simple solutions of other times – the state for some, the corporation for others – more on the basis of resistance and fear in the face of the transformations under way than because we actually believe in the regulating power of these instruments. No one with a normal level of ethics and common sense is comfortable with this new world. And the concern is not restricted to the left. A truly productive businessman – not those who control the global casinos – may believe that he is defending free enterprise, but with every company that closes down or is bought up by some institutional investor, he is left with more doubts. And when they compare their profits, the result of real efforts and risks, with the fortunes won by speculators with the money of others, including government money funded by their own taxes, they start to have doubts about the very logic of the system. Are the pay scales of chief executive officers in big corporations proportionate to what they bring into the economy?

Gut feelings probably still rule our emotions when we take sides in the great duel between state and corporation that characterized the twentieth century. But the understanding is gradually emerging that we need to build new perspectives. It is no longer a simple left–right polarization that informs the concern so well summed up by Ignacio Ramonet, in *Le Monde Diplomatique*:

> In the next ten years, two opposing trends will probably play an important role in the planet. On the one hand, the interests of large globalized companies, driven by financial interests, which draw on techno-science with an exclusive spirit of profit. On the other hand, an aspiration to ethics, to responsibility and to a more just development that takes into account environmental demands, which are vital to the future of humanity.

Social development, environment, ethics, the central role of culture, and other concepts emerge in a confused but powerful manner in this new problematization of human development. In this extremely turbulent and threatening universe, the search emerges for a more humane society. The new directions don't belong to any one particular class; nor are choices between traditional divides – left or right, liberal or conservative – sufficient to turn our society around.

We face a complex analytical process, because reality advances swiftly, and the challenges we face are renewed on a daily basis. It is a rocky path, full of pitfalls. But it has to be travelled, because our traditional and enduring intellectual bunkers, which offer comfort to the extent that we reinforce them with dogma from the past, are no longer sustainable. The course of the war has changed, or, as Octávio Ianni says, *a política mudou de lugar,* the place of politics has changed.

The point, therefore, is not to discuss some macro-theoretical alternative, but rather to place on the table some of the new cards that we have to play. It may no doubt be called a 'third way'. But the concept of the third way is misguided if it assumes that there were ever only two ways, and simplistic if it is meant to bring about a pleasant *ménage à trois* of corporate power, a bureaucratic state and civil society, in which contradictions will have disappeared. In fact, the world is evolving along other paths, without being overly concerned with the simplistic concepts with which the twentieth century tried to hobble it. Today there is a third way, tomorrow there will be a fourth. Good politics demands enough flexibility to ensure a permanent process of democratic change, constructing ever-new realities, and not some kind of final destination, be it Gidden's 'third way' or the idiotic 'end of history'.

It would be easier if there were a catechism in economics, but there isn't. I suggest that the reader treat the notes below not as simplified rules, but as points of reference to assess directions of change. Most of them are obvious, and I am attempting not to be original but, in correlating some key ideas, to see if we can make out some emerging shapes. To be honest, these ideas are fairly simple, and are already part of our daily lives in one way or another.

Points of Reference

From a grand clockwork to a complex society

One approach is to wait for an inspired theory that will make sense of everything, the kind of theory of everything physicists are working on. Another is to ask if there is any sense in the current system. In other words, is there a globally intelligible mechanism, or are we really only a mishmash of interests that interact in a chaotic and unpredictable manner? In fact, beyond a given number of variables and dynamics, predictability becomes limited. Some years ago someone asked me where I thought Nicaragua was headed. I, as a planning adviser at the centre of government, should have had some idea. In fact, it is not a question of having information and a suitable theory of interpretation: it has to do with the fact that the number of variables, in this case ranging from the corruption of the Contras to the electoral cycle of the United States and internal squabbles within the Nicaraguan oligarchies, along with possible volcanic eruptions, obliged us to have a radical modesty in terms of analysis, and to seek a scientific evaluation of the very *comprehensibility* of the emerging situations. It isn't a matter of bowing to the unpredictability of things or of appealing to the impotence of theory. It is the conviction that we, in this era of transformations, need a shock of interpretive modesty. At the same time, a minimum of realism and of information about what is happening on the planet convinces us that, with our increasingly powerful technologies, constructing coherent trends has become a question of survival.

From the grand vision to viable alternatives

This modesty doesn't mean inaction, but rather a change of focus. In a sense, it is no longer a matter of defining the ideal society, a *good* utopia, and fighting to create the political space for its realization. As Ximena de la Barra, a long-time fighter for children's rights, commented ironically, humanity will not stop at a given moment to adopt a new system that appeals to us. We are increasingly seeking actions that are *evidently useful* or *constructive,* such as distribution of income, improvements in education and other initiatives that correspond to the relatively obvious values of dignity and quality of life. At the same time, when we identify critical trends in our development – global warming, destruction of the seas, social exclusion of the weakest members of society – we seek to create counter-movements. A pragmatic school of political action is thereby developing. Many people can be mobilized and organized around the objective of, for example, ensuring that in a given city every child is well fed, has shoes on their feet and a place in school. This focus is not necessarily 'micro'. On the contrary, it creates possibilities for actions by any citizen, through individual initiatives, as well as through groups, neighbourhoods and associations, in pursuit of the so-called *common good.* And by revealing resistances to change, it makes the political options and necessary structural changes more evident. It is an insufficient but necessary condition for the construction of a broader policy. And it is about recovering the civic dimension of politics and the force of the everyday life of the common citizen, overcoming the fatigue that frequently afflicts those who await the grand utopia, the ideal political party, the great leader, or the so-called objective conditions.

The integration of economic, social and environmental objectives

On the other hand, focusing on economic growth and expecting the rest to follow, through some sort of 'trickle down' magic, is not realistic, and is part of the utopia of natural balances, the conservative version of social illusions. An understanding of the *common good* is becoming reasonably widespread. Social justice is not the natural result of economic efficiency, nor is respect for the environment. Similarly, to try to centre everything on social justice without ensuring the economic resources for social investments makes little sense. And of course, neither the social nor the economic activities will make any sense if we continue to destroy the planet. The overall objective is thus summarized in this simple formula that we find today in United Nations documents: we need a development that is economically viable, socially just, and environmentally sustainable. To achieve one of the objectives without the others simply doesn't resolve the problem. And it's no use saying that the current system is less bad than the others: is it less bad to fall from the fifteenth floor than from the twentieth?

Bridging the state, the private sector and civil society

The integration and articulation of these economic, social and environmental objectives will not miraculously occur thanks to the good will of corporations, which are today focused on profit at any cost, or by some miraculous recovery of the capacity of the state to act, or even through the relatively fragile organizations of civil society. The very irruption of organized civil society into the political arena doubtlessly resulted from the increasingly widespread feeling that neither the macrostructures of state power nor the macrostructures of private power are responding to the prosaic needs of society in terms of quality of life, respect for the environment, generation of a climate of security, or preservation of a space for liberty and for individual and social creativity. In the succinct formulation of Claus Offe, the battle has raged for too long between those who demand all power to the state, preach a comprehensive privatization with unrestricted corporate power, or sing the praises of a poetic and all-embracing 'small is beautiful', replete with alternative communities and technologies. The first gave us the communist mess, the second gave us the social tragedies of so-called neoliberalism – once a ready-made argument for the communist alternative – and the third is essential but not sufficient for the political equilibrium of society. The key word here is clearly the *integration* or *articulation* of the various instruments for change. We are condemned to integrate in a reasonably balanced manner the powers of the state, of corporations and of civil society organizations, and the vision of political solutions centred on privatization or on statism amount today to unsustainable simplifications.

I am personally convinced Giddens did us all a great favour. We do have to go beyond the traditional right and left, and to open up space for a new vision of politics. If the traditional political right uses the 'third way' to put a smiling mask on its old face, we are not in the realm of political ideas, but of political tricks. We must criticize the tricks, and the persons who condone them, but not the need and the attempts to seek new visions. And the really new idea is the direct organization of civil society around its interests, pressuring both state and corporations for a deep change in the overall organization of society. This can be deeply and constructively revolutionary.

Social objectives and democratic rights: from charity to participation

It is not sufficient to achieve the defined social objectives: it is also necessary to achieve them in a democratic manner. In other words, the articulation of state, corporations and civil society around the larger objectives is not simply a matter of technical efficiency. In abandoning the vision of the finished utopia, and opting for the permanent construction and reconstruction of our social objectives, we choose democratic means of decision-making as a central element in the construction of objectives. It is not sufficient that a company, or the state, does something that is good for the population. The point is to understand that the right to construct one's own future, and not only to receive useful things in the form of a 'favour', whether from the state or from corporations, is an essential one. No political or economic actor has the right to impose anything on us, with the argument that it is for our own good, without giving us the institutional instruments to inform ourselves, to express our opinion, and to participate in the decision-making process. In this regard, the reality is that the current forms of decision-making of the state, and of private corporations, are extremely similar in their tendency to transform the citizen into a passive and manipulated subject. Civic participation is an essential question in these current transformations.

Corporate control: from diffused power to hierarchical power

The moment we are going through is one of an overwhelming dominance of 'big business'. This is the only force that is coordinated at the global level, and it dominates many decision-making mechanisms of national states, controls the financial instruments of representation of human wealth, and maintains a positive image of itself though the power it exerts over the systems of communication. Prior to the rise of the global corporation, the multiplicity of productive companies ensured some degree of democracy in political decisions of society, because power was more dispersed. Today, some economic mega-actors behave like owners of the planet – the Gateses, Bertelsmanns, Murdochs, Turners, Soroses and others – creating a sort of transnational social group, to use the formula of Leon Pomer. Faced with this reality, all that remains for the rest of us mere mortals is our fragile rights of citizenship every four years, broad impotence and political discouragement, or simply social exclusion, in the case of the around 3.5 billion people in miserable conditions who make up two thirds of the population of the planet. This organized and coordinated power of the mega-corporations seeks to present itself as the simple servant of the market: the so-called market forces are presented as anonymous, and thus democratic, subjecting all to their will. In fact it is a political power, highly structured, which generates dramatic imbalances in the global economy, while accountable to no one, because it presents itself as being no one – it is 'the market'. And of course any attempt to limit its excesses is an attack on 'the market'. Clearly, in the state–corporations–civil society relationship, big business is the segment that completely throws out of balance the process of social development.

Big business is not a vague and negative notion. Actually, some 500–600 corporations dominate the end products in key areas like finance, media, information technology or pharmaceuticals, and have been using global connectivity to spread their power. They are responsible for the bulk of the US$450 billion spent annually on advertisements, a massive image-building effort that gives them, besides, huge leverage over all the media, particularly the news system, the so-called free press. It is important to understand that this sets them apart in the economic system. The mechanic next door is a private company, but makes little politics, and his brand building is the satisfaction of the neighbourhood with his work. Mega-corporations cloak themselves in the legitimacy of the market, but in reality they are powerful systems of media, financial and political manipulation. In other words, it is nowadays too gross an approach to speak simply of private companies, or of capitalists as owners of means of production. Jack Welch, presenting his 'surprise' at being chosen as chief executive officer of General Electric, writes, in *Straight from the Gut*, that he had no particular relationship with the financial and political milieu. Because this is the *work* of the manager of 'big business'. Enron was basically about politics, as are the corporations that presently are being chosen for Iraqi projects.

The weakening of the state

Under these conditions, it is not surprising how fast the traditional forms of politics are being discredited in the eyes of the population. In the United States, a president is elected with less than one quarter of the votes of the country, and the votes he obtains are largely won through millions of dollars in funding by corporations – by 'the market'. *Business Week* once commented that the support of Rupert Murdoch was 'instrumental' in maintaining conservatives in power for two decades in England. Was Murdoch elected? The very fact that many economic processes have shifted to the international arena, in the context of 'globalization', makes the state largely impotent in the face of the great global movements of financial speculation, concentration of income, and environmental destruction. Furthermore, essential to the survival of an elected government is to keep on the good side of the large economic groups. And this means playing their game, under the threat of being deprived of investment, or being the target of speculative financial attacks or campaigns by the great global media groups. We consider it normal for a bank merger to create a financial group with US$700 billion in capital. Speculative transfers exceed US$1.5 trillion per day. A mere half dozen large countries account for a trillion and a half dollars in production of goods and services per year. Brazil, eleventh-ranked economic power of the world, has foreign currency reserves of less than US$30 billion. In Joel Kurtzman's metaphor, today the tail wags the dog. Thus the state is co-opted, and has lost its capacity to serve as a political counterweight, and to balance economic, social and environmental objectives. The great corporations, in a moment of post-communist euphoria, created a broad privatization movement, blaming the state for all evils. This tendency has been seen as a danger for the entire process of social reproduction, not just by the left, but also by a growing group of social actors from a broad political spectrum. With the rapid erosion of governance all over the planet, it is no longer only the excluded who are at risk.

Counterweight of civil society

Perhaps the most significant change in the potential for new directions comes from an understanding of the role of organized civil society, or civil society organizations – the non-governmental organizations (NGOs), community-based organizations (CBOs), non-profit organizations, Third Sector, etcetera. Their presence is rather limited in developing countries. In the United States, they employ 15 million persons. Around 80 per cent of Americans belong to some kind of association, and more than 100 million Americans report having done some kind of voluntary work in an average year. In strictly economic terms, we are talking about a contribution to the US GDP of around US$700 billion from this sector alone, compared to a total Brazilian

GDP of around US$500 billion. On the whole, this sector is relatively strong and widespread in developed countries, and weak in poor countries, where politics is reduced to the traditional duo of private and state oligarchies. With technology ensuring a new culture of connectivity, combined with urbanization, which favours local organization, an immense space has been created for modernization and democratization of political, economic and social management, especially through local participatory systems. For the purposes of this analysis, the key point is that the inadequacy of the big corporations and of the current forms of centralized state organization, in terms of their capacity to respond to the fundamental needs of society, is increasingly leading society itself to roll up its sleeves and pursue the necessary activities in new ways.

There is an interesting convergence to be seen in the works of Manuel Castells on the network society, Robert Putnam on social capital, Lester Salamon on the Third Sector, Lawrence Lessig on the control of information, and Hazel Henderson on the power of non-monetary economic activity and of collaborative arrangements: the huge potential for social organization at the roots of society.

State division of power, and social bridging of power

To situate the discussion in the context of integration of social forces is a step forward. In recent Brazilian history, the classical approach has been to discuss the problem in terms of the relations between the three powers, with debates over more executive power for the Presidential system, more legislative power for the Parliamentary system, and control of the Judiciary by the other two powers. Civil society normally enters the debate through the little door of political parties, and solutions to lost political legitimacy are sought in directions such as district voting systems or campaign finance reform. Since the problems are never resolved, we can always claim that Brazilians don't know how to vote. As for the private sector, the big corporations disguise their organized political power, and appear only as campaign contributors, along with the 'lobbies', in Brazil a polite term for systemic corruption. Placing the discussion at the level of the social division of power is more interesting. It involves formally recognizing the (real) political power of corporations, and the (necessary) political power of organized civil society. It involves recovering the capacity of the state to organize the new social pact that the nation needs, and strengthen it. It involves taking the large corporations out of the ministries, out of Congress and out of the Judiciary, thereby 'de-privatizing' the state. Finally, it involves stimulating the organization of civil society so that it can perform its watchdog role *vis-à-vis* the state and the private sector, and the recovery of a minimum of a culture of social solidarity without which neither the economy nor the political system will be viable. In this new context, the debate shifts from obsessive discussion about whether power is best left in the hands of the corporate or the political oligarchies, and places the problem at the level of the relation between economic power, political power and civil society.

From the manipulated society to the informed society

To call what we have in Brazil a democracy involves a strong dose of goodwill. Since our history has involved long periods of dictatorship, we react like a peasant who was obliged to bring a goat into his hut – when the goat was removed, he felt a huge sense of relief, and his hut seemed quite pleasant. But the peasant remains a peasant, and the house continues being a hut. To transcend the 'politics of the goat' and get to a politics of consistent social progress, society needs to be duly informed. This in turn means the democratization of control over the public means of communication – the media. In this sense it appears important, in particular for the democratic forces that have focused their objectives on economic alternatives, to recognize the centrality of cultural processes and communication. The traditional pillars of oligarchic power – arms and money – have been complemented by access to media control, and the impressive possibility of permeating every home, every waiting room and every bar with the incessant message about what we should think about everything and how we should run faster to have more success. The volume of pseudo-information that is forced upon us has become a central social and political fact. We mentioned above the US$450 billion a year advertising represents worldwide; this goes up to one trillion if we take the advertising and marketing industries together. It takes up hours of our daily lives, and invades a great portion of this extremely limited and precious resource – our capacity for conscious attention – with an incredible amount of rubbish.[5] Thus, more or less implicitly, influence is exercised over the opinions and values of the vast majority of the population, forming a kind of intellectual inertia that blunts any new idea, any generous impulse, any different thought. We come to desire that which is expected of us. Today, much more important than discussing control of a steel mill or state monopolies is the discussion of how to reduce the monopoly over the media. It is clearly not a question of transferring media control to the state, replacing one monopoly by another. The key is to ensure a multiplicity and wealth of diverse and decentralized sources of information, along the lines of networks: the Internet already points us to new paradigms in social organization. Information and communication, and the transparency that both make possible, constitute the instruments *par excellence* of the participation of civil society in the political process, and the essential element in ensuring coherence of the whole.

UNESCO's *World Information Report 1997/98* notes that information is one of the fundamental rights of citizens – not least because, without the necessary information, citizens have no way to exercise their other rights – and it should be provided in a public manner and free of charge. The *World Summit on the Information Society*, in 2003, gave us all a magnified view of how central this process has become to the reorganization of society. The big media corporations explained, during the Summit, their efforts to generate an informed society. But the reality is that our communities are daily informed on the details of

---

[5] Even so conservative a publication as *The Economist* states that 'people are tiring of ads in all their forms', and that 'consumers' resistance to the growing intrusiveness of marketing and advertising has been pushed to an all-time high' – *The Economist*, Special Report on the future of advertising, 26 June 2004, p. 71.

Michael Jackson's problems with young people, but, if we organize a community radio to coordinate development efforts in a *favela*, we are immediately invaded by the police, on the grounds of 'piracy'. So we know everything about Michael Jackson, and nothing about our neighbourhood initiatives or development options, not to speak of local cultural creativity. Speak of a free press!

From pyramids to networks

Our vision of social organization continues to be based on the pyramid, on the system we inherited from the Vatican or from Roman legions, in which one gives orders to two, who in turn give orders to four, and so on, with the growing complexity being faced with the multiplication of levels. But we know that after a certain number of hierarchical levels the top of the pyramid comes to have only the delusion that someone is executing its decisions, and the base has only the delusion that someone is rationally managing the process. In reality nothing works. Health care, for example, is a community-based service that has to reach every citizen in all regions of the country. It is what we call a 'capillary' system. For the system to operate from a centralized command in Brasilia, with dozens of levels and the corresponding complexity, is simply an administrative impossibility. The reason we have an oligarchy is not necessarily that the people don't know how to vote or because we are intrinsically corrupt. The complexity, the rate of change and diversity of situations of a modern society make the old Roman or Prussian verticality outdated. Hierarchy, with the multiplication of levels and centralization of decisions, naturally excludes the base. Deprived of control from the base, that is, from the population with a stake in the decisions, the system is literally out of control. This can be felt at the level of political loss of governance, as well as at the level of corporate loss of governance, in the giant chaotic private bureaucracies.

On the other hand, with the increasingly urbanized populations, forming organized spaces at the grassroots of society, we see the prospects for a radical decentralization and democratization of the ways we manage our affairs. In another era, this could lead to a breakdown of the broader political system. Today, the new systems of information and communication permit the system to be decentralized and to function in a network, replacing much of the hierarchy of command by horizontal coordination and information density. This paradigm shift has already penetrated a range of corporate areas – with both positive and negative aspects – and constitutes the working philosophy of many civil society organizations, although it has taken only the first steps in our vision how we organize political institutions.

The diversity of institutional solutions

A society organized in a network, in an information-rich environment, may become more open to flexible institutional solutions that are constantly being rebuilt, thus avoiding standardized solutions that seek to fit different situations into the same format. It is a matter of articulating a range of organizational solutions, and no longer choosing between the radical simplifications of state or corporation. Different areas of activity also demand different solutions. The market can be a competent and useful regulation mechanism in some areas, particularly for material production; but it is essential to have control over productive activities that involve heavy use of non-renewable natural resources, and others that lend themselves readily to cartels. The infrastructure sector, especially in areas like energy, water and transportation, demands a strong state role, because these areas require extensive investments, with very long payback periods, and with economically diffuse effects; this type of activity demands long-term planning, to make sure the system is coherent. The social area, including education, health care, culture, communication and sports, works poorly with traditional state bureaucracy, and worse with profit-centred bureaucracies. It is enough to see the disaster of private health insurance, the explosion of curative medicine at the cost of prevention, and other trends that directly affect our quality of life. In this area, there is no state bureaucracy or private profit that can ensure adequate regulation: what is necessary is the strong presence of an organized community. Thus the problem is not one of choosing between state or private property, according to traditional ideological options, but of constructing appropriate relationships between the state, corporations and community, on the one hand, and the various levels of governments – national, state and local – on the other. It is also not enough to look merely at the property dimension, since a hospital could be private *property*, with *management* by a non-profit community organization, *controlled* by a council of citizens within the framework of state government *regulations*. Or it could be a state hospital, managed by a private group, under the control of a municipal council. This type of articulation doesn't always fit within our ideological pigeon holes, but this is surely the direction we need to evolve towards if we are to recover the social utility of our efforts. If the new technologies offer any positive potential, it is exactly that of a new and much more flexible management, adapted to different conditions. We are moving towards an articulation of diversified mechanisms of regulation. The all-encompassing privatization envisioned by the neoliberals is just as extremist as the wholesale nationalization attempted by the communists. The manic pursuit of privatization is understandable because of the profits it generates, but it is indefensible in a modern social vision.

Urbanization and the spatial dimension of social objectives

If the solutions are diversified, and modern reality more complex and fluid (because of the very speed of the current transformations), at some level the different initiatives should be accounted for in terms of results, or what has been called quality of life – the objective, after all, that justifies these efforts. The city, whether we like it or not, has become the basic unit of institutional structure and of our social life, and it must assume its integrative function for a range of initiatives, whether they emanate from the private sector, the state or civil society. It makes no sense for the state to plant trees, beautify the city and dredge rivers, while industries discharge chemicals and developers occupy wetlands and deforest hillsides. Initiatives that come from institutions pursuing completely different objectives will not contribute to the synergic construction of social objectives, unless there are institutions that allow the creation of convergences and synergies. A private company will seek high efficiency in microeconomic terms, because if it is not efficient it will close: it has to adapt to an external control, which is the sanction of consumer interest. A city, for its part, has to seek a minimum of efficiency, which we could call 'social productivity', to avoid, for example, the absurdity of a city like São Paulo being paralysed because of an excess of means of transport.

The city has achieved 'modernity' only to have its residents travel at an average of less than 10 miles an hour, inside machines that cost tens of thousands of dollars and were built to travel at more than 100 miles an hour. The fact that everyone knows the technical solutions to the problem forces us to rethink the way we manage our decisions. Leaving aside monster cities the size of São Paulo, which constitute a reality unto themselves, the fact is that the city constitutes the basic unit where the private economy, the social policies of the state at its various levels, civil society, environmental objectives, the networks formed to address critical poverty, integrated policies for jobs and other objectives, can all articulate around a proposal that has both head and tail. And it is becoming increasingly clear that, as some activities become more global, we need to reinforce that anchor that we have under our feet – local management of our resources. Organizing the rationality of city management, in the broadest sense of productivity of our efforts and quality of our lives, can thus become a cornerstone for social organization, bridging micro and macro economic objectives.

New tools for governance

Brazil has been carrying out some interesting experiments in public administration. The *Conselho de Desenvolvimento Econômico e Social* (CDES) allows the key actors in the economy – unions, bankers, the Movimento dos Sem Terra (landless movement), key industrialists, influential academics – to get together and to negotiate new solutions. What the government is doing enriches the fabric of control of civil society over the state and the economic area, overcoming the absurd alternative that is offered to us of being controlled by public or private monopolies. Ove Pedersen provides studies of what he calls 'negotiated economy' in the system that is emerging in the Scandinavian countries:

> The system of comprehensive political cooperation is much more than an instrument for decision making and coordination of a polycentric whole and of various levels of institutions. The entire system can be seen as an institutional prerequisite for a negotiated economy. A negotiated economy, therefore, can be defined as an instrument for structuring of society where an essential part of the allocation of resources is conducted through a comprehensive system of political cooperation between independent centres of decision making in the state, in organizations and in financial institutions.

We have already had some test cases in Brazil, with the 'Sectoral Committees', and the already famous participatory budgeting, launched in Porto Alegre and now applied in a great number of cities in Brazil and abroad. The resistance that emerged is understandable, given the composition and backwardness of the private and state oligarchies in Brazil. Traditional city councillors do not like the use of money being directly decided by the residents of a neighbourhood. However, a new political and administrative culture is emerging, with a new understanding of civic participation and of the very functions of politics, which probably has little to do with the pure models of the state or the corporation. It is no longer a matter of the 'victory' of one over the other, but rather of the emergence of new trends that draw to some extent on both, and on new organized spheres of power. The general mistrust of so many people concerning the vote as an instrument of political participation is fully justified. People know that the vote isn't sufficient anymore. Big business certainly behaves as if there were no limits, but will suffer a powerful backlash as we face an increasingly chaotic situation in economic, social and environmental terms. And the participation of business in the construction of a more balanced political system is just as necessary. In fact, it is a new kind of institutional architecture we are looking for.

Classes, social actors and civic involvement

This new approach implies rethinking the concepts we use to define social actors. The twentieth century was marked by a messianic vision of redemptive classes: bourgeois in the capitalist vision, and proletariat in the socialist one. Since the condition of each class depends on its role in the production process, everything was centred on the opposition between who is the owner of the factory and who works in it; who gets the profit and who earns a wage. The centrality of the factory in production processes is fading quickly, following in the footsteps of agriculture, with some decades between them. And the complexity of economic subsystems that form in the actually existing economy is such that to speak of macro-categories of this type is to risk oversimplification. The role of a social group in the production process is still important in informing political positions, but it doesn't have the centrality it once had. Today there is a richer and more complex interaction of traditional class divisions with attitudes that result from more or less narrow professional self-interest, with regional roots (belonging to a neighbourhood, a community, a city, a linguistic minority, or other influences that result not from the space of work, but from the space of residence, in the framework of what John Friedmann calls the 'life space'), and other components of cultural identity. All this frequently leads us to the uncomfortable sensation that defining ourselves as left or right is insufficient, because the various moments of ideological definition intersect in a diversity of ways. And again, the concept of civic participation, and the universality of human rights coexisting with a diversity of individual or social expression, comes to play a prominent role.

'Us' and 'them': the ethical divide

These new trends give us a feeling of ambiguity when we try to define the groups we identify with. In discussing a society that has to seek more complex arrangements for social interaction, balancing the diversity of social actors and the universality of human rights, we easily agree that things really have become more complex. However, when we open the newspaper and see the picture of a certain kind of politician, we know perfectly well where we are *not*, the vision of the world with which we *don't* identify. The world, in a certain sense, becomes simple again. Where is this border that doesn't exactly represent a rational understanding of different classes, but is rather an intuitive *gestalt* that tells us that we *know* which side we are on? Jordi Borja provides a very clear definition of this divide: there are politicians, businesspeople, journalists, heads of a wide variety of churches, hosts of television programmes, jurists and other actors whose political influence results from an organized appeal to that which throws one human against another, like racism, revenge rather than justice, xenophobia, male chauvinism, the arrogance of wealth, competition at all levels, ridicule and disparaging of the weakest, or simply of the different, etcetera; and there are political projects that seek to reinforce the most generous qualities of humanity, drawing on the values of solidarity, tolerance, respect for difference and social justice. In general, the first option, that of playing on human weaknesses, tends to be the easiest way of conducting politics and of articulating social forces. People can feel appreciated when they see their darker side stimulated. It is a style of politics, economics, media and culture that appeals to the gut. Playing on fear and insecurity is a marvellous political instrument. The most advanced communication technologies have become an impressive instrument for the promotion of political backwardness.

It is striking how, despite the sophistication of our intellectual capacity, we manage to simplify our political positions. The cynic values cynicism, and explains that humanity is worthless, thereby lending some philosophical respectability to his own lack of decency. The idealist frequently seeks an ideal of a decent human being, and thus frequently lapses into complete disillusionment. We can say that the human being is neither good nor bad, or that he is both. Actually, this is not the point. The important issue for those who seek practical solutions to make this world better is that there are forms of social organization that tend to bring forward the positive dimensions in us, and others, which played a key role in creating fascisms and dictatorships, which feed the 'beast' and seek in it their political strength.

I read once in a Sunday newspaper an article full of blatant falsehoods about an African country which I happened to know well. I was struck by the number of people who happily accepted and repeated the rubbish, undeterred by the obvious lies in the article. To confirm people's prejudices makes a journalist popular, much more so than describing the problematic realities. The crucial point here is that this watershed can be complex, and can cut across and divide unions, parties, associations, and newsrooms. In any case, it cannot be reduced to the traditional division between left and right, or between one class and another, and is not determined by the role in the production process alone. Understanding this division has become essential, given that issues ranging from planetary survival to satisfaction with our everyday life now demand a new social ethic. This ethic, in turn, cannot materialize without the convergence of social actors sustaining it. The reinvention of a social humanism, which was once treated as a manifestation of an impotent idealism, is today a crucial necessity.

An example of this trend can be seen in the annual publication of the *Human Development Report* by the United Nations, focusing on indicators of quality of life, in contrast to the older *World Development Report* of the World Bank, based on GDP and financial activities. More recently, initiatives like the Calvert–Henderson indicators, focusing on a wide range of economic, social and environmental results, have broadened the debate. This trend is also reflected in the corporate environmentalist movement, and in the new emphasis on social responsibility for economic activities. When we speak of the general disillusionment with politics, we are forgetting that we cannot reduce politics to party politics and government. Actually, politics confined within a narrow conception of political institutions tends to degenerate in the absence of control and guidance from civil society: this emphasizes the need for a constructive search for more democratic forms of social and political organization.

From the ethical divide to the power of corruption

The consciousness within civil society of our ethical divide is being fed by the broad sense of indignation and impotence that we all feel in one way or another. It is not a matter of moralistic hand-wringing, but of a perplexity, an uncertainty, about how to face the extremely sophisticated systems of corruption that dominate political, economic and judicial spaces, and the media that inform us about them. We all have this sense of the existence of a dark and viscous universe of interests at the centre of private and public power – a space that predominantly coincides with the political right in general, but goes beyond this divide and beyond the implicit simplification of 'good' and 'bad' classes.

In other words, it is natural to have different and contradictory interests in society. We are learning to cope rationally with the fact that workers, business people, small producers and others have divergent or convergent interests depending on the issues, and that it is legitimate, if not necessary, to coordinate them. But that is not the issue here. What is at stake is a mafia-style manner of coordinating and negotiating interests, which has little to do with capitalism or the market, and because of which any real articulation or negotiation becomes extremely difficult, preventing the already difficult construction of another social and political culture.

This issue is addressed in a very ineffectual manner in Brazil. The reality is that there is systemic corruption, which involves the highest levels of political and corporate power. We are not referring here to some corrupt individuals who interfere with the normal procedures of politics. We are referring to political and corporate activities themselves, organized in a manner that serves to divert and appropriate public resources, which will be used to finance private contracts, to fuel contributions to ever more expensive campaigns, and to leverage access to new spaces of power. We are dealing with the political force of a system that, for example, scandalously inflates the costs of large public works projects, creating fabulous profits for the contractors, who for their part contribute millions in kickbacks for the campaigns of corrupt candidates, who will vote for new projects with over-inflated budgets. There are millions of dollars in 'loans' to owners of huge rural properties, which will later be converted to millions in subsidies. There is the blackmail of the banker who liquidizes billions of dollars in operations with friends, and then calmly awaits the bail-out from the government, because a country cannot let the system collapse, especially because the bankers make these deals with the money of the citizens, and not with their own resources. And there is the scandalous way in which radio and television concessions have been handed out, allowing these same politicians and business owners to present their perspective on a daily basis to a completely disoriented population, which will then be accused of not knowing how to vote.

This point is particularly important in Brazil, because it is one thing to discuss whether the neoliberal vision is or is not appropriate for the country, but quite another thing when the theoretical arguments are merely smokescreens for a permanent system of organizing govern-ment and business decisions around corrupt interests. There is no possibility of organizing and coordinating new and different policies, nor of institutionalizing government practices, when the differences don't even reach the political level, and when the political space is seen by dominant groups as an instrument for promoting their own interests. The newspapers show us every day what this is costing us. But more serious than the direct cost of diverted resources is the corruption of political processes and the corrosion of democratic legitimacy that is generated along the way.

It is, in the technical sense of the term, a mafia-like system, where solidarity and co-responsibility between the corrupted and the cor-ruptors generate networks of power that penetrate the hierarchies of the legislative, executive and judicial branches of government, blocking any formal capacity for government. Cities, states and broad segments of the federal government are managed through dense networks of contractors, corrupt politicians, real estate speculators and supportive media, along with a scandalously complicit judiciary.

The network of solidarity in illegal activity naturally generates a closed system of self-interest and ensures silence. It should be remembered that it is practically inevitable, in any society, to have occasional political corruption and corporate fraud, as a marginal element of the system. This type of activity ends up being detected and rooted out, since it involves minorities that obstruct the work of the other professional members of the institutions. But when the corruption becomes systemic, it is the professional minority that that ends up being co-opted or expelled by the mafia. How could one expect the São Paulo city councillors, for example, to judge the criminal activities of their members when the majority participated in them?

It is important to remember that despite beautiful books like *Os Donos do Poder* ('The Owners of Power') and other sociological essays about the general character of the Brazilian ruling class, there has been no analysis of the concrete family structure of political and economic power in Brazil, or of the arrangements that renew and reproduce it. In the actually existing Brazil, it is the same parallel structure of power, if not the same families, that have been governing the country. They continue holding on to real power, by threatening the business community with the absurd but effective blackmail of the possibility of a progressive government, and assuring landowners that they are the only ones willing to be brutal enough to protect them from agrarian reform, and playing on the eternal fear of the elites that one day the masses will rise up in response to the oppression and humiliation they suffer. Thus the very misery generated in the country, by these same elites, preserves a broad moderate buffer around it, and prevents the opening up of any space for a vision of renewal. Even when an exception arises, as with the election of Lula, the new government has to walk in the very narrow space it has opened in the traditional structure of densely meshed interests.

This alliance of moderate business interests with a mafia-like structure of power is the basic reason that today Brazil has the most unjust distribution of income on the planet, that we can't manage to feed the people in a land so blessed with natural resources, and that we are tossed around by financial speculation schemes like any banana republic. The truth is that this mafia-like power structure, and the systemic corruption that sustains it, renders impotent any effort towards reform of the state, institutional modernization, or evolution towards a civilized society.

Here, as in other areas, we need a strong dose of realism. Even if we have a formal democracy, we are dominated by corrupt systems that have little to do with democracy. So before we discuss the various facets of neoliberalism, social democracy or socialism, we have to face the tougher task of recovering our very capacity to construct political options. This task demands the participation of a political spectrum much broader than the existing left in Brazil.

Political projects and economic workings

This internal difficulty is further complicated by changes in the international context. No matter how attractive it sounds, a vision that integrates the state, private sector and civil society, in pursuit of an economically viable, socially just and environmentally sustainable society, collides with the evident fact that the economy has become in large part global, while the political instruments continue national. And governments, as we have seen, even though elected by parties of different orientations, today largely take the approach of aligning themselves with the demands of the global financial system, out of the simple need to survive, and not be crushed by the global system. It is strange to see how confused the line is between people and social actors who defend the most nationalist positions and those who celebrate globalization. We find people who would never have anything to do with each other defending similar arguments.

And one should not forget the paradox of a left that was once accused of being internationalist, materialist, atheist, and contrary to moral and family values, and which now sees these supposed objectives being vigorously pursued by the dominant economic and cultural forces, in the name of diametrically opposed ideals. Today, it is globalization that is corroding the nation, while 'the market' is taking away people's property and savings, the media are feeding us obsessive consumption, corporate clout is reducing the space for individual initiatives, and so on. Thus, the conservative vision becomes increasingly incoherent, and there is a growing perplexity in political spheres. It is striking to see the former Prime Minister of France, Raymond Barre, one of the most traditional professors of economics at the Sorbonne and proponent of conservative economic theory, making the following observation: 'We can certainly no longer leave the world in the hands of an irresponsible band of thirty-year-olds who think only about making money.'

Global capitalism and national legitimacy

Identifying the space where construction of a socially and environmentally viable economy can take place thus becomes a key problem. How do we construct national, regional and local political projects, within a political and economic context managed by actors that operate at the global level, beyond the reach of social and environmental controls? How do we bring about the necessary transformations within a power structure supported by an environment of systemic corruption? At the same time that the objectives – environmental, social and economic – become clearer, therefore, the chances of achieving them become more remote. For developed countries, the problem is less stark, because they benefit from the economic advantages of an imbalanced global division of labour. Developing countries, however, face a double weakness: they are too powerless in economic terms to influence the directions of the global economy, or even to have room in which to manoeuvre; and at the same time they are characterized by privileged oligarchies surrounded by a sea of misery, with consequently limited internal political legitimacy. Thus oligarchic interests tend to depend on external support. The essential limitation is thus located not in individuals, but in a context. These governments cannot face simultaneously the domestic tensions – directly linked to the social apartheid on which their power is based – and the external confrontations that are indispensable to a firm negotiation of their political space in the global economy. The nation's internal cohesion and the government's legitimacy are fundamental factors for the renegotiation of external relations. A situation is thus created where the only way for a government to recover space to manoeuvre within the global economy is to confront domestic social apartheid. Contrary to the neoliberal dogma, in today's world sound social policy means sound economic policy, which in turn opens political space for a sound international policy.

From exploitation of labour to global poverty

The problems have deepened to such an extent that a sound approach (as opposed to mere rhetoric) to achieving social equilibrium could actually expand international legitimacy, which is more and more important in today's world. We expect economic processes to provide goods and services – that is, *products* – but also *income* for the various participants so that they can purchase these products, and *work* for everyone, because without work there is no income and no citizenship. At the centre of the political debate we still face the key weakness of capitalism: it is a solid organizer of production, especially if the company is free to organize itself without bureaucratic obstacles, but it is a terrible distributor of income, and it is increasingly a mediocre creator of jobs. Since the cycle of reproduction involves both production and distribution – otherwise the whole doesn't function – capitalism is structurally incomplete. To abolish the business organization would be to throw the baby out with the bath water. To fail to face the problem of income and employment in an institutionally organized manner is irresponsible. Cosmetic speeches aside, the reality is that we are reaching the economic and political limits of social stability. The World Bank figures show that 2.8 billion inhabitants, almost half the world population, live on less than US$2 a day. More than 150 million children go hungry in the world. More than 800 million are illiterate, and the number is growing. Today the world produces more than US$5,000-worth in goods and services per inhabitant, enough for all to live with comfort and dignity if there were a minimum of good sense in the distributive processes. With the immense economic and technological resources we have at our disposal, this situation appears just as absurd and anachronistic as slavery and colonialism. A United Nations (1997) report sums up the issue well: 'No longer inevitable, poverty should be relegated to history – along with slavery, colonialism and nuclear warfare.' The report characterizes as 'obscene' the wealth of the 447 individuals in the world who have a personal fortune greater than the income of the poorest half of the global population. An understanding of these contradictions is ceasing to be a privilege of the left, and is bringing together people from a wide range of social and political areas.

Unlimited growth and limited resources

This retreat from the neoliberal free-for-all is also being strengthened by environmental dynamics. The case of the oceans is a good example: with the global positioning system (GPS), modern sonars and the other paraphernalia of industrial fishing, the uppermost image is certainly nearer to a slaughterhouse than Moby Dick. With more fish supply on the market, one would assume that a fall in prices, and a resulting reduction in the catch, would bring the process into balance again. This is what used to happen when markets worked. But today, with the size of the global catch rapidly reducing the total biomass, supply is dropping, and prices are rising. In other words, the cost of catching fish is dropping thanks to new technologies, but prices are rising due to the growing scarcity of production. Thus margins rise, and instead of restricting fishing to ensure the survival of the raw material, the large fishing companies put all the equipment they have out to sea. The argument that they are destroying their own future is met with the laconic reply of 'if we don't do it, others will'. In other words, the traditional supply and demand curves never meet, until the fish stocks are destroyed. For areas that don't produce their own product, but rather exploit the reserves accumulated by nature, market mechanisms, in combination with new technologies, become a form of suicide. The same logic, which once eliminated the bison on the

North American plains, is now, with the help of aircraft and more advanced technologies, eliminating the millions of reindeer and other animals from Siberia, principally to produce dog food for sale in developed countries. In other areas, the system follows a logic of *externalities*, through which it is cheaper, in market terms, to produce while discharging toxic effluents in rivers, thus destroying the limited supplies of clean water, than to pay the costs of recycling or treatment, or a less destructive production system. The problems are piling up at such a rate that the range of social actors willing to apply the brakes on the process is increasing rapidly, which also expands the spaces for broader political and institutional architectures. This is not just wishful thinking. Ten years ago environmentalists were still seen as a curiosity, like tree-huggers and whale-lovers. Today these concerns are widespread.

From relations of production to the content of production

The relations of production were at one time the focus of indignation because of the social injustices involved in the distribution of income between profits and salaries. This process continues in great part. But today money is made selling arms to any part of the planet, laundering money from drug trafficking in the most respected banks, selling human organs, organizing sex tourism and child prostitution, selling mercury that poisons rivers, flooding naive (or just irresponsible) farmers with chemicals, pushing fast food and soft drinks into schools and generating an epidemic of child obesity, over-fishing throughout the planet, burning off millennia-old forests to expand pasture, exploiting the most sordid facets of human suffering in media programmes, inflating the costs of public works through contractors, selling the services of criminals as security services, providing private military services to weakened governments, etcetera. A preliminary survey of companies that produce torture equipment found 42 companies in the United States, 13 in Germany, 7 in France, 6 in Taiwan and 5 in Israel, among others. It is not sufficient today to know if a company pays well or poorly, if they respect labour laws, if they are creating jobs or not, if the legal formalities of business organization are being respected. It has become indispensable today to discuss the social objectives of productive processes, through the media, unions, political parties, NGOs, and business organizations themselves. Companies linked to socially useful activities will be the first to pay the costs of the passive solidarity that links them – as colleagues, so to speak – to those who exploit legal, political and social weaknesses. What legitimacy does the United States have to protest against Colombian drug producers, for example, when they have recently quadrupled arms exports to African countries? Flooding poor African countries with arms is more ethical?

Jobs: a new hierarchy

Modern management literature loves 'showcases'. When we read the publications, it seems that the business world is being invaded by a wave of internal humanization, with reduction of hierarchical levels, promotion of the 'knowledge organization', reengineering, Kan Ban, Kaizen, TQM (total quality management) and other components of the global alphabet soup. On the whole these proposals are frequently positive. However, they are an attribute of a narrow group of modern corporations. One must remember that the transnational corporations employ 12 million people in all the Third World. The International Labour Organization, which publishes these figures, considers that every direct job generates another indirect one, which gives a total of 24 million, or around 1 per cent of the economically active population of the underdeveloped world. Indeed, this leading edge minority sector does generate jobs, but of another type, known as 'precarious jobs': Nike employs 8,000 persons in the United States as 'organizers', working with the *intangible* products that characterize the modern economy – advertising, accounting, design, lawyering and the like – while the actual tennis shoes are produced through outsourcing systems in Asian countries, with the famous 20 cents per hour wages. The profits are concentrated in the United States, the precarious jobs spread in Asia, and the products invade every country, generating unemployment, for example in the shoe industry of Franca, in the state of São Paulo. This unemployment in turn generates an immense informal sector, where people attempt to earn a living through micro-industry activities in their garage or basement, small-scale commerce, and so on. Finally, it creates a rapidly growing illegal sector that thrives on such activities and products as stolen cars and parts, smuggling, money laundering, drug production and trafficking, deforestation and illegal fishing, or traffic in organs and blood.

Thus our working world is progressively separating into socio-economic subsystems, with the leading sector prosperous and modern, while the manual labour is carried out in the precarious sector, the informal sector and the illegal sector, a hierarchy that can be found in industry, agriculture, commerce, mining and any other area. We cannot allow ourselves to be hypnotized by the advances of Bill Gates or Jack Welch, and ignore the elimination of decent employment opportunities for the vast majority of the world's population. Here, bringing some balance back to the chaos being generated by the fact that we have an overwhelming dominance of large corporations, a general weakening of the state, and a civil society that is still the junior partner of the process, is a task that will involve a systematic search for ways to strengthen the organizational density of society. In this regard, it is useful to see our society as one in transition: market mechanisms have already ceased to function in a number of areas, and have given way to coordinated processes of the 'managed market' – when not simply monopolies and organized manipulation of markets – and the social instruments of management are still at a very early stage of development.

From material production to intangibles

The technological revolution has made management from a distance more viable, generating gigantic systems which coordinate thousands of production units. Thus production activities are still important, but the power over production systems has shifted to the core unit that coordinates finance, distribution, advertising, public relations, lobby-ing, legal services and other 'intangible' elements that today represent somewhere around 75 per cent of the price we pay for a product. This power has shifted largely to the transnational sphere, out of reach of national policies. A positive image of this highly centralized power is artificially built through gigantic campaigns, and the power of this process can be seen in such cases as Enron, a scientific showcase for *Harvard Business Review* and so many other opinion makers, yet so hollow. A powerful company all too often doesn't produce anything; instead it controls, sets rules, and creates fee systems that give it vast powers of intermediation. David Korten and others refer to 'intangibles', *Business Week* to 'The Land of the Fee', Jeremy Rifkin to 'the age of access'; in my books I have used the image of a 'toll-booth economy'. All this affects the potential and directions of social transformation. In particular, the broad power of a great corporation is not exercised in the concrete space of a plant, the neighbourhood where its workers live, or in the traditional system that generates much of our urban social fabric. The large company is today a name: it reinforces its image on a daily basis through all the communication channels, but its concrete existence we recognize only on the supermarket shelves.

And the power to control the intangible activities leads to a qualitatively new appropriation of the wealth that a society produces. Peugeot, in the first half of 1998, had profits of US$330 million, which was celebrated as an achievement by the 140,000 workers who produce concrete goods. In a similar period, in the first half of 1997, Citibank, with 350 operators for foreign exchange speculation, made US$552 million in profits.

The traditional business owner who develops innovative production processes, believing in Schumpeter's creative destruction, feels more and more like a fool when seeing where the profits go. The traditional process through which increased profits meant more investment, hence more jobs and stimulation of the economy, is changing. UNCTAD's 1997 *World Trade and Development Report* summarizes the problem well: 'It is this association of increased profits with stagnated investment, growing unemployment and falling salaries that constitutes the true cause for concern.'

The economy and social services

An area with great potential to organize civil society is the area of social services, which have acquired much more weight in the economy than traditional industrial activities. Many are still surprised by the fact that the largest economic sector today in the United States is not the automobile industry or the military complex, but health care, which accounts for 15 per cent of the US GDP, which in dollar terms is more than Brazil's total GDP. Another giant that exceeds the great industrial sectors is the entertainment industry. However, when talking about management models, we still talk about Taylorism, Fordism and Toyotism. Our entire vision of economic organization continues to be centred on the automobile. What does 'just in time' production mean for a hospital or a school? These great new sectors swing back and forth between state bureaucratism and the shocking abuses that the private sector commits when it moves into the social areas. The thousands of young people who show deep scars from kidney extractions in India, and the 52 per cent caesarian births in the state of São Paulo remind us to what extent companies are committed to their greatest objective, profit. How 'free to choose' is a person when a doctor says his child should have an operation, preferably in a private clinic with which the doctor is associated, even if the cost is not covered by the patient's health insurance? What 'market' is this? As the main axis of our activities shifts to social policies – health, education, culture and so on – social organization will necessarily change.

The most significant development areas today are those sectors where neither the state bureaucratic paradigm nor that of factory organization apply. An analysis of non-profit organizations in the United States shows that around 50 per cent of their activities involve health. The US$200 billion that the US government spends on the Third Sector in health alone results from public tendering processes that non-profit organizations win – at the expense of corporations – simply because they are more efficient. This new phenomenon of 'social corporations' has been more extensively studied in Italy, but is gaining ground all over the world. Whoever said that building more effective organizations can only occur in a capitalist 'free-for-all' context? The reality is that the essential part of human activities is shifting to areas where the state macro-bureaucracy and corporate macro-power both function poorly, thus opening a wide avenue for grassroots organization around the growing new social sectors.

From manufacture to knowledge economy

We all live under the general assumption that productivity stems from competition. This view is being hammered into our brains constantly through the different means of communication. Competition certainly does rule, but less and less through market mechanisms. Cutthroat competition does not mean that corporations are playing by market rules, or seeking advantage through better service to the consumer. The capacity of markets to bring order into economic activity is dwindling rapidly, as typically half a dozen giants rule the different economic sectors, managing the system through strategic agreements. The invisible hand is also losing its grip as the core of economic power shifts from material production to intangibles (accounting, marketing, lawyering…) and the content of production shifts to social services. But if we step a little backwards, the common denominator of this change is that the knowledge content of everything we do is rapidly increasing, as we evolve towards what has been called the information society. This means we have to face the institutional implications of a knowledge economy.

To have economic value, things have to be useful to people. But for a corporation to earn money, things also have to be scarce. Air is useful, but plentiful, and therefore has no economic value. Beaches are plentiful, so they have no economic value, unless we manage to close one, making access to this pleasure scarce, so that we can make people pay for it. Knowledge certainly is useful. The difference between manufactured goods and knowledge is that we have to make sure goods are recognized as our property so that we can sell them, and get money in exchange, with which to purchase other products.

The key issue, as Alvin Toffler has shown us, is that knowledge is different: if we give manufactured goods away, we won't have them any more, but if we share our knowledge it still remains with us. We will have shared it, and the sum of knowledge in society will have become bigger.

To make knowledge pay, on the other hand, we must make it scarce. Thus the private property/competition paradigm that ruled the world of material production is becoming a factor of scarcity in the knowledge economy. There, the collaboration paradigm is what works, simply because it makes knowledge more accessible. Once a factor of productive advancement, private property and competition, the locked secret has become a factor of backwardness, as feudal property had become a limitation on the growth of markets in other times.

A *Business Week* cover story cites a very interesting example: how is it that Linux, developed and constantly improved by thousands of voluntary contributions, delivers a better product than Microsoft, with its flood of money (to which we all contribute), the best information architects, an army of lawyers, and a secretive environment of guards and patents? Simply because knowledge is something to which we can all contribute. And – probably a proof of our utmost perversity – not only do we do it for free, but even with pleasure!

It is not surprising that big corporations put up a gigantic battle at the World Trade Organization (WTO) to guarantee them intellectual property rights on virtually anything that smells of creativity, or resembles an idea. The patented right to the 'one click' granted to Amazon is a huge monument to the absurd application of manufacturing era regulations being forced upon the knowledge economy. Genentech patented fundamental technology needed for the artificial synthesis of antibodies in 1989. Playing on minor changes, Genentech obtained an extension of the patent expiration date to 2018, which means it sits on a technological area for 29 years, waiting for royalties from whoever wants to produce research and development in the area. This is what we have called a toll-booth economy.

From global space to local space

Social services have a privileged sphere of action – local space. Thus, if, on the whole, the balance being constructed between market, state and civil society needs to reinforce the weakened poles – the state and civil society – an important role is created for the municipality or local authority, where coordination between public administration and civil society organizations can more easily be effected.

It is at the local level that health, education, sport, culture and other policies can be integrated in dynamic synergies around the quality of life of the citizen. It is at the local level that the register of unemployed can be compared with under-utilized resources to create employment policies. It is also at the local level that the various social actors meet each other, allowing partnerships to be formed in the most flexible manner.

I won't dwell on this point, which I have analysed elsewhere. It should be remembered that we are dealing with a dynamic that has worked itself out in several global contexts, especially in the Scandinavian countries, Canada, Holland and elsewhere, but also in very poor regions like the Indian State of Kerala, which made a profound transition from centralized representative democracy to a participatory democracy much closer to the citizen.

In developed countries, local administrations manage between 40 and 60 per cent of the public resources, while in underdeveloped countries this percentage is generally lower than 10 per cent. In Sweden it is 72 per cent, and in Brazil about 13 per cent. The point is to bring the state down to the level where its interactions with social needs and civil society organizations can become stronger. This will not be accomplished simply by wishful thinking. Brazilian politics being what they are, the decentralization of resources could simply strengthen local political chieftains. But, on the whole, it is much easier for large corporations to divert billions of dollars through the ministerial lobbies in Brasilia than to face the social pressure for concrete actions in the more than 5,500 municipalities in Brazil.

Corporate power and citizen power

Establishing more democratic and balanced social relations and containing corporate power has always been studied from the perspective of democratization of control of corporations, involving approaches ranging from outright socialization of the means of production to the counterweight of organized labour in factories. The first solution has showed its obvious limitations, while the second continues to be a very important objective. But another strong candidate has emerged – that of citizens voting with their wallets, so to speak, by refusing products that are prejudicial to the environment or that are produced with child labour, in order to penalize companies with unacceptable social behaviour. In other words, the influence on production processes could occur in various points of the cycle, and in more complex ways than simply transforming property relations. The collapse of Shell's sales in Germany after the accusation of negative environmental behaviour is very significant here. The Lyon Summit on Partnerships for Development, organized by the United Nations in 1998, included two straight days of presentations on alternatives being adopted in various countries, regions and communities to restore social control over savings and so subvert the schemes by which they are appropriated by the globalized financial system. Local communication systems have developed rapidly, as a counterweight to a global pasteurization imposed by the media monopolies, and have resulted in new instruments for local cultural integration. Again, a clear implication is the need to democratize media, at the broadest level, so that the population has access to appropriate information, including information about corporate behaviour. Another important implication is that individual economic behaviour does matter, voting with our pockets every day, so to speak, without waiting for the big alternatives.

The new dimension of social time

Finally, it is important to underline another issue: the dramatic acceleration of planetary transformations obliges us to rethink the concept of time. The evolution of a group of companies towards management of quality, reduction of hierarchies and greater internal democracy, for example, holds promise. But what about the cleavage with the rest of society, which evolved at another pace? This kind of company represents 5 per cent at most of global employment, and little more than 1 per cent in Third World countries. Almost half the population of the world still cooks using firewood. What about the two thirds of the population excluded from the positive aspects of modernity, but included in such impacts as unemployment, rising prices of medicine and concentration of wealth in a shrinking planet? The problem here is that it is not enough to think about the modern leading edge which *may* one day reach a broader social basis: the social and environmental imbalances are mounting, and the window of time that we have to re-establish certain structural equilibria is limited. The *asynchronies* of the processes of change are so deep, imposing different tempos on technological time, cultural time, institutional time and legal time, to mention some basic processes, that the threat of disastrous disintegration, along the lines of what has been called 'slow motion catastrophe', becomes more and more concrete.

It exemplifies this tension, which exists on different levels, that São Paulo has increased the number of companies certified under ISO-9000, ISO-14000 and other certificates of modernity in this era of technological medals, while, at the same time, we have 30 murders and 420 cars stolen per day, marking the rapid growth of an illegal economy which is no longer the sporadic manifestation of social marginality, but an entire economic sector and a systemic process of bottom-up social disintegration. The new trends of modernity receive all our attention, and command almost all the content of scientific publications. We should undoubtedly be happy about the fact that corporations do a lot of business. However, if the time of reorganization of society around our activities doesn't match the pace of social disintegration, the outcome will be barbarity. The time we have for a solid reorganization and balancing of society is increasingly short.

The Focus for Action: Bridging Exclusion

Many see the tragedies occurring around us as a natural outcome of the birth of a new world. We all look to the brilliant horizon filled with fantastic technologies. It is relatively easy to envisage the golden future that these technologies are preparing for us. Alvin Toffler, in his book *Powershift*, pointed to the fact that an economy based on knowledge is essentially different from a society based on control of material wealth: knowledge passed to another person is shared, while material goods belong to one person *or* another. Thus, there is the possibility of the construction of a democratic society, structurally more egalitarian. Pierre Lévy shows, in *Collective Intelligence*, how the horizontal connectivity that new systems of communication and information allow, creates spaces for innovative social arrangements.

In other words, we can analyse a range of manifestations of these new trends: Rifkin points to the end of work, Castells to the networked society, De Masi to a society of creative leisure, Lessig to the endangered information commons, and many other authors paint future nirvanas where we will be delivered into leisure and pleasure while robots do our work for us; meanwhile, yet other, more pessimistic authors show us a human being subsumed under Big Brother; and there is every possible shade in between. These studies are important, because they focus on directions, on macro-trends. But what is essential now is to understand the more immediate processes in which we can intervene.

The immediate issue is the chaotic transition we are entering. If we stand back and gain a bit of perspective on the industrial revolution, we see its birth was accompanied by de-ruralization, the formation of urban slums, of huge migrations to the New World, immense misery, child labour and so many other phenomena that are forgotten today but which traumatized the nineteenth century and the first half of the twentieth. The very force of communism and the radical expropriation of the capitalists in communist regimes emerged from these social tragedies, which left the legacy of the Cold War and the climate of planetary conflict.

So the problem is not the emergence of the fantastic futures that the new technologies promise. To produce more with less effort should not be of concern to us: the threat is the replacement of the worker without corresponding advances in the reorganization of work. How to redistribute work, and reduce the widespread suffering? How to integrate the excluded three quarters of the global population into the transformation process?

Will the corporate power, presenting itself as the 'market', resolve the issue? The statistical fact is that it is aggravating it. In fact, better than discussing whether the liberal or neoliberal theories provide a response is to propose a practical alternative: let us start in an organized way, community by community, region by region, to address the problem of millions of children going hungry or without school; to create minimum income programmes; to devise links between communities and the decision-making processes for public resources; to control arms proliferation; to eliminate environmental destruction; to restore the control of individuals over their own savings; to vote with our wallets for socially and environmentally responsible companies; to elect honest politicians; to stimulate local and community communication systems; and to promote responsibility.

The transition to an industrial society nourished immense tragedies in the twentieth century. The greater earthquake that is creating the knowledge society could become either a process of liberation, or a universe of terror. Cristovam Buarque points out that our society as a whole is starting to get tired of the polarization of income, violence and corruption, and that the abolition of misery, for which we have both the technical and economic means, is today as prominent an issue as was the abolition of slavery at the end of the nineteenth century. We cannot continue to create privileges while closing our eyes to the consequences. In the economy, as in politics, it doesn't help to pretend that all is well.

New Game, New Rules

Let us come back to where we started. It appears to me essential to realize that we are to a large extent playing a new game, but still trying to use the old rules. We need to reconstitute our conceptual approach. Some of the cards that make up the new deck should be privileged. This approach overcomes the nationalization/privatization debate, and instead focuses on the balanced coordination of the state/private sector/civil society. It seeks to transcend the priority given to the economy, and the failed vision that the profits of the rich will result in social and environmental benefits for the whole society, through the magic of 'trickling down'. The very process of social reproduction should be a permanent integration of economic, social and environmental objectives. This focus on 'organized society' is crucial in the face of a capitalism of large global groups, which today escape any national control by the weakening state economic policy instruments, while global controls have still not been created. This 'total capitalism' today exercises an immense power over the political arena, and controls the media, which enables the constant dissemination of a positive image of the system while hiding the crises that are piling up. Since the global financial system is also largely free of national controls, a profound imbalance is created between the state, market and civil society. We face the central problem of recovering the regulatory function of the state, and of strengthening the organization of civil society, as well as generating international institutions that can work.

Simply hoping that things will 'naturally' find their own logic isn't enough. The capitalist tide raises the large yachts, but it does not raise all boats. The economic polarization between rich and poor is clearly recognized by all the international reports, both within and between countries, and today it is especially strong in the United States itself. The capacity to create jobs is changing rapidly in the leading sector of the economy. If the approach to development is centred on 'attracting' investments, with each country or region competing to see who can stoop the lowest, and give the most attractive benefits in exchange for a few hundred jobs, in what the United Nations now calls the 'race to the bottom', it isn't going to get us anywhere we want to be. In fact, what works is just the opposite – stimulating job creation around basic needs such as sanitation, housing and food, the redistribution of productive land, and more democratic access to income, with external relations seen as important but as complementing the internal dynamic. After half a century of falling further behind developed countries, it is up to us now to centre policies on social and economic inclusion, and on finding new arrangements with the global economy.

The formation of a mega-power made up of 500 to 600 transnational corporations has shifted the spaces for politics. The business community itself, especially in the area of small and medium-sized business, lacking the magnitude to control segments of the political sphere, and unable to participate in the global casino, is increasingly bewildered by a system where producing well doesn't ensure any advantage relative to those engaging in financial speculation, manipulation of the state, or imposing fees for a broad range of activities.

On the other hand, the pervasive urbanization that has transformed the planet, and in particular Brazil in recent decades, creates new prospects for the reconstruction of state/civil society coordination within the space of the city, allowing (but not guaranteeing) the generation of an economic and social anchor, which is increasingly necessary as globalization advances.

One of the great dilemmas continues to be this strange creature that we call Brazil's ruling class. Its ideological adaptation to the era of globalization is relatively simple, because as a class it always sought to maximize its own returns through intermediating external interests, whether colonial, English, American or transnational. We were the last country to abolish slavery, and we are today in last place in terms of distribution of income. Recently Darcy Ribeiro has offered this eloquent assessment in his *O Povo Brasileiro* (*The Brazilian People*):

> Nothing has been more continuous nor as permanent, over these five centuries, than this dominant class, exogenous and unfaithful to its people.... Everything, over the centuries, was in constant transformation. Only this dominant class remained the same, exercising its interminable hegemony ... Here they haven't achieved even the lesser feat of creating a prosperity which can be shared with the working masses, as was achieved under the same regimes in other areas. They have had even less success in their efforts to integrate into industrial civilization. Today, their intention is to force us into a marginal position in the new emerging civilization.

To imagine such perverse intentions is perhaps an exaggeration. There is an old saying that before blaming perverse intentions, one should first exhaust the immense possibilities of simple stupidity. But our reality remains perverse, even in the context of dramatic technological advances and the dizzy pace of change in all areas. Our banks continue to depend on government finances and charge outrageous interest rates; the sugar mill operators and huge landowners concentrate on what they consider to be politically smart – seeking subsidies through their covert pressure and locking up land that they don't cultivate or let anyone else cultivate; contractors support corrupt politicians in exchange for government contracts; media families loyally follow the corrupt traditions of Assis Chateaubriand, controlling information and media space in order to perpetuate their political and economic fiefdoms; the clannish organization of politics continues to exact its dues and protect its own. All of this constitutes a baroque power structure, barely hidden behind the cellphones, computers and luxury cars of the ruling class. Brazilian capitalism has managed an impressive feat: it has left everything unchanged, pulling a shiny technological mask over frozen and corrupt political relations.

It is easy to wind up an analysis of a situation by criticizing the ruling groups, by identifying a culprit. But the great fact is that the conservative vision of the world has little to give us. As we saw above, the market and globalization fail to ensure even the space for individual realization, or a supportive social context for families, while eroding national sovereignty and other traditional values. Thus, the neoliberal vision of the economy has become incompatible with the values that were associated with it. It is not surprising any more to see a conservative Pope castigating savage capitalism one day, and defending Pinochet the next. The conservative vision has become a contradiction in terms, and its compass spins aimlessly.

The progressive vision, for so long encased in the statist vision of society, is now opening up new spaces for the renewal of society as a whole. The idea of a participatory democracy, anchored in decentralized systems of social management, and based on the free access to information and culture, clears the way for a politically coherent system, because it is based on a balanced coordination of the actually existing social forces. The vision of partnerships between the public administration, the private sector and civil society is an advance that is proving its effectiveness in many countries, although in Brazil it has only moved forward at the local level. The pursuit of democratization of media to create transparency in the use of state and corporate resources is one more pillar of a healthy civic culture. It is no surprise that the concrete alternatives are emerging principally from local governments: this is the space where the political, economic, social and cultural spheres can be integrated to form a coherent whole. This does not mean a society whose logic is reduced to the local level. But it does mean that a society coordinated in a democratic manner at the community level can better ensure the rational coordination of the whole.

We frequently orient our actions more as a function of the ideological universe to which we belong than in terms of their social utility. In my view, the social, political, economic and environmental problems have reached a point where discussing them at this level has become pointless. What is important is not the ideological shade of each idea, but whether the new arrangements that are gradually emerging open up the new paths we need to follow. And a minimum of information on what is happening with the environment, poverty, violence and despair throughout the world shows us that the time-window we have is not very large.

As I am reviewing this translation, I see a smiling George Bush (the kid) promising on television that in a decade man will tread on Mars. I personally think that his government is already in orbit. There will be a time for Mars. We should rather concentrate on being able to tread safely on our old earth.

PART 3

The Mosaic Reconstructed

To judge by the comments of friends, the pages above have been read with great interest in the more biographical part, some impatience with the more analytical arguments, and an amused interest regarding the ethical comments, of the 'life's little lessons' sort. In fact, we all want to live a full life, we are passionate about our passions, we all learn little lessons, and thereby gradually assemble the mosaic of our values. We do have to use analytical tools, sometimes in the anguish of incomprehension, forced by the need to understand the world. The richest path is not always the easiest one.

Important as theoretical rigour is, however, it doesn't appear to be sufficient. A broader problem could be identified by asking how to reconstruct the unity of the mosaic. Is it natural for our lives to be so fragmented? To be broken into scattered moments of a gesture of kindness, of madness in traffic, of a mechanical 'I love you too', of growling like mad dogs in professional disputes?

We could turn everything around, and pose a simpler question: what is important? And as a function of this question, we could rethink love, friends, sociability, work, creativity, and also – why not? – the economy.

The unity of the recomposed mosaic, of the whole figure, is undoubtedly given by love, by friendship, by solidarity; by the countless facets of affectivity that make us family, society, culture; by what transforms the fractured times of our everyday life into a space where art and work, for example, can find their common sphere in creative work, instead of being placed into hermetically sealed compartments: diversion in one space, sacrifice in the other.

This may sound like a dream. Paulo Freire, who never had the slightest fear of dreaming, said that his goal was a *less wicked* society. Personally, I think that this society, centred on money at any cost, where the rich can't sleep because of fear, and the poor because the rich don't let them, and where all live in fear of tomorrow – this when the world produces wealth and technologies that would allow peace and comfort for all if there was a minimum of redistributive decency – truly has to rethink the path it is on. The combination of an unbalanced power structure, of deformed and manipulated market mechanisms, of an idiotic ideology of success and an unchecked materialist consumerism has led us to an impasse in terms of life, of the simple day-to-day existence, of prosaic personal happiness.

And this is not just a question of theories. When the neoliberal ideology pursues the purity of its economic principles and forgets to think about the impact on our everyday lives, it simply takes us back to the law of the jungle, even if it shows off complicated equations. Science, when divorced from values, can be dangerous. And we are all, in a sense, condemned to enter the game, because we simply have to earn our living. When resources are finite, and the social product goes to whoever can grab it first, or more brutally, we naturally slide towards barbarity.

Institutions and Schizophrenia

Let us go back to Eilat, in the gulf of Aqaba, on the border between Jordan and Israel. The year is 1963. Pauline, at 17, worked in the Maar Ka Shva – the Queen of Sheba – a luxurious international hotel. She sold jewellery at a small counter in the hotel. Her letters from Brazil were opened. But the hotel was full of successful people, like those we see in all the photographs of luxurious hotels. Pauline had a dazzling smile, because she was in front of *clients*, and not people with joys and sadness like herself. And the instructions were clear: the salary was proportional to sales, and the smile had to be dazzling. Sometimes when I see the dazzling and fixed smiles of young women presenting some programme on television, I worry that at any moment they might have facial cramps. Isn't it 'economic' to be a person whose smile is less conspicuous?

I recently saw a documentary about Cuba, focusing on the recovery of tourism there, a completely different kind of tourism. People go there not because of the beautiful swimming pools, or the waiters in traditional dress, but because they can talk to people different from themselves. For visiting French or Americans, these Cubans are persons with whom they can talk as equals, in a relation that is not mediated by one's interlocutory function in a hotel for the successful: on one side a source of money, called the client, and on the other a recipient of money. Why would I prefer the waiter to show a long face, if he has a problem, so that I could ask, as if he were a real person: *que pasa, Manolo?* What a lack of professionalism, to let one's personal problems interfere, failing to create distinct and fragmented personalities within ourselves!... The worldwide success of *Buena Vista Social Club* wasn't the result of transforming common people into artists, but of showing artists as the real people they are.

We have become so accustomed to all this, that it doesn't even appear important. But what is the cost of fragmenting a person into professional and personal dimensions? Anyone who has painted his entire body for carnival knows that, covered in paint, the body doesn't breathe and becomes asphyxiated. And what happens when we paint ourselves every day when we leave home with this monument of artificiality that increasingly clashes with who we really are, and which leads us finally to the couch of the analyst who is paid to hear us as we are? So, at the right price, we can buy three hours of authenticity per week.

The past is alive in us, even if we don't always remember it. When I met Pauline again, as she was leaving her hotel, I was shocked by her huge smile, which was the same size as the accumulated unhappiness of that year of solitude and artificiality she had gone through. The girl I had met in Brazil, with her striking 16 years, smiled at that time with a disarming spontaneity, without a thought or care behind it. It was a true smile. But what I now saw in front of me was a huge smile, suspended in a sea of sadness. Today, almost forty years later, I still feel all the cruelty of a social process in which all the spontaneous experience, the explosion of life, was tamed, civilized, put within its 'proper limits'.

In the first part of this little study I briefly described this episode. In reality, Pauline sought in me a salvation that she was not able to achieve on her own. She was like a broken person, and wasn't able to recover the spontaneity and intensity that we had lived through before, or to reconstruct the relationship from the memories that had stayed with her, less and less animated, in those nights of solitude. We were two solitary persons, looking at each other, an abyss in our eyes, because it wasn't a relation that could be content with pretending, and the spontaneity had been swept away by the expectations imposed on the relationship.

After a few days, I thought of going to Tel Aviv to try to find some way for us to make a living. On the way I turned back and arrived earlier than we had arranged. Pauline was in a coma – she couldn't stand the sadness and had tried to commit suicide. I spent three days with her in the hospital, in her slow and painful return to life. Her first words, only semi-conscious, were full of desperation: I don't want to come back....

We were just kids, but so much more mature. What did we care about the executives with their briefcases, radiating success, or the women with the breasts full of silicone? What is the significance of all the success in the world, compared with a girl who fears returning to life? We managed to overcome this phase, to rebuild our lives. The human individual is both fragile and strong. I would survive, and she would die, years later, at the hands of the Brazilian military. But from that point on, both of us had an exposed raw nerve – an awareness of the absurdity of things, a yearning for human solidarity.

To criticize the civilization model we live under (please forgive the pompous term) is not easy. At some point along the way to this present we lost our North, our sense of what is and is not important – and became immersed in a war of successes and significances that is best understood as a social farce. Socially powerless in terms of our own lives, we seek to cover with varnishes of various types, with external and ridiculous symbols of success, our tragic loss of humanity and the immense solitude that we accumulate within ourselves.

The problem with the economy could be the rate of growth of GDP, but society's problem is that the GDP is not sufficient. And the key problem is society – we human beings – and not the economy. The economy has to go back to being what it really is: just a means, and not an end. Keynes expressed it so gently: 'If economists could manage to get themselves thought of as humble, competent people, on a level with dentists, that would be splendid!'

The great global corporations that manage us are unarguably competent in technical terms, but a tragedy in terms of human sensibility, in terms of their cultural and political contribution to society. There is a very simple reason for this: each manager, each director within each corporation wants to prove that he or she is the most efficient, and the common measure is money. If a director manages to sell a medicine at a higher price because advertising makes it more attractive, he or she will shine at the board meeting, when showing off the rising profit curve. The declining curve of the number of persons who have access to the medicine is not shown, of course; more significantly, it wouldn't have any impact on the success of the director if it were. The system creates a negative natural selection, a biased process of decision making.

Jack Welch was a success. His *Straight from the Gut,* with a title so full of sincerity, mentions the importance of ethics every two or three pages, but General Electric's record is an endless list of trials for fraud, environmental crimes and the like. This is not a game; our lives are at stake. My son Alexander, with the cool irreverence and rather greater sincerity of the young, had a short comment: 'straight from the butt'.

Once again, the technical human being is separated from the ethical human being, thereby creating isolated compartments within ourselves. We sleep with parallel personalities within us, which try to ignore each other because they are contradictory. We become, in the most rigorous sense of the term, schizophrenics. Who hasn't seen interviews in which the manufacturers of small arms – designed to be concealed and to kill people – explain indignantly: 'I don't pull the trigger…'?

We are quite powerless in the process. It was pathetic to see executives from the large tobacco companies before the US Senate, each one testifying, with a serious face, to his personal conviction that nicotine isn't addictive. Gunnar Myrdal, in *An American Dilemma*, a monumental book written in the 1940s that earned him the Nobel prize, asks how there can coexist, in separate parts of the American conscience, a universe of values that preaches liberty – that says 'give us your poor, your tired, your huddled masses' and supports individual achievement and human rights – and at the same time a universe that allows that same American to go out at night and burn the houses of people of another colour? Today they don't burn houses, or the houses they burn are not in the US, anyhow; the style has changed. But the dilemma remains.

The loss of ethics in the modern corporation, and in the day-to-day behaviour we have to adopt in earning a living, is much more than macroeconomic idiocy. It means a loss of our direction as a civilization, an intimate corruption of ourselves, our families, and our children. In the final accounting, when we sacrifice social happiness to pursue individual success within a corporate microcosm, we are betraying ourselves, and ensuring our unhappiness, because the sense of the absurdity of our lives lies within us, eating away at us from the inside. Discussing the manipulation of news in the press, an American journalist was asked about the possible feelings of a young reporter who would legitimately want to succeed in his career, but be honest in his information: 'Well,' he said, 'you have to choose, it's either integrity, or the job.'

One lives life in its entirety. The social dimensions of individual happiness are essential. When we feel unhappy, torn apart by contradictory motivations, incapable of creating coherent lives in an absurd context, we manage to convince ourselves that we are the guilty party. Analysts, with honourable exceptions, won't hesitate to explain the deep, and of course individual, roots. Because if we talked about the social roots, where would we end up?

Identities

Israel is undoubtedly an efficient economy. But it is sinking in a sea of hatreds. The hatreds are social processes, but they also appear in individual attitudes. Pauline's father preferred to see her dead rather than going with a miserable *goy*. We are talking about people with a university education and money, who speak several languages, who know which glass is for wine and which is for water.

Good sense would tell you the following: the persecution of the Jews in Europe – and the comfortable solution of arranging another place for them to live, a place which happened to be a geographic area that was already inhabited – was tragic. The persecution and expulsion of the Palestinians by the Jews is just as tragic. The two peoples had lived there for thousands of years, and if it is a question of precedents of this type, we should expel the Americans and Brazilians and return the land to the native Americans.

When the Soviet empire collapsed, the Russian minister of foreign relations said jokingly to the US President that not having an external enemy would be a terrible blow for the American government. The foreign enemy was maintained. Successive presidents raised other threats, other Satans, to hypnotize television viewers: Saddam Hussein was a memorable Satan, with his black moustache; Fidel, too, with his beard, although he's not very convincing as a threat to humanity any more; the Serbs were great, even though it was difficult to hide the reciprocity of the massacres and violence. Qadhafi was useful for some time, Khomeini was impressive, and there will be others. The atrocious massacres in Chechnya, which a decade before would have outraged the world because Chechnya would have been a victim of the Soviets, now don't even make the news, because those behind the massacres have become our friends, and an arrangement has been negotiated, leaving a free hand to Russia in Chechnya, and a free hand to the US in Iraq.

The feeling of belonging to a group, nation, civilization, religion or race flourishes admirably if we have an opposing pole, a negative mirror, the detestable image of those who *don't belong*. In Orwell's *Nineteen Eighty-Four*, we had the hateful figure of Goldstein. In religions, some sway standing, others kneel, others sit, and each group considers itself the elect, the chosen people. In Africa, they even dance. If an extraterrestrial enemy was to invade, perhaps we would plant our feet on the ground, and realize that we are simply human beings, lost on a small blue ball in space.

It is, once again, a natural feeling. When we send a child off to school, we think that he or she is well dressed. We are bemused by the child's distress if the shorts are not the right length, if the sneakers are not of a certain type, if the shirt happens to have buttons – or doesn't have, depending on the school and the environment. This demonstrates our immense need to assert our identity, and our immense fear, from a young age, of being *different*. The apparent slovenliness of a teenager's clothes is painstakingly constructed. When I walk around my university, I can tell from a long way off if a student is in Law, in spite of apparent differences among them. The impression given by the clothes is as clear as a military uniform, men or women. I am not throwing the first stone: many eyeglasses used by economists could be patented.

The genius of the system of the large corporation is that it doesn't require bad people. It just requires people who are socially docile, and individually ambitious. It demands people who construct their identity not around solidarity – identification with others – but around superiority. My car is bigger than yours, my house is more expensive, my salary is bigger. The game of identity, coexistence and solidarity is transformed into a fight between winners and losers, in which neither side will ever be satisfied, because we do not know what we are fighting for. More profit? A bigger stone on our grave?

Identity and Culture

We are cultural beings, and culture is a social process. In cultural processes, rational motivations come into play rather seldom. Or in any case much less often than we think. And culture is also much more powerful than we imagine. We are all racing around and working ourselves to death, and no one stops to ask: where are we running to?

Andres Duany, an urbanist who dispensed with developers and contractors (remember *The Truman Show* – it was filmed in a suburb of Panama City, Florida, designed by him), began to develop communities that mixed residences and services, where one doesn't need to be enslaved to the car, with small spaces agreeable to day-to-day life, and pedestrian-friendly neighbourhoods, where there is less emphasis on showing off the individual success of the owner than on reinforcing the community environment. 'Success,' says Duany, 'doesn't consist only of saying "My house shows more good taste," but rather "My daughter has more friends than before."'

We are all getting increasingly tired of a life full of cars, violence, waste and pollution. However, the mega-corporations that influence politics and global economic trends also control the means of communication, and systematically orient our behaviour towards a civilization of competition, the rat race, domination, success, and unchecked consumerism. It is so much easier to manipulate the consumer than to innovate in the processes and content of production, not to speak of institutional change.

The logic of the process doesn't require us to be against companies or economic activities, but rather to make clear that economic activities cannot be ruled only by profit. Without a solid counterweight of organized civil society, that stresses the prosaic interest of our gross domestic happiness, we will be heading quickly towards a catastrophe in the social, environmental and economic spheres.

The way we organize our daily life appears to us as *our* options, and the advertising messages always insist on how these are *our* choices, and how they are *natural*. If they were so natural, they wouldn't require billions of dollars in publicity to convince us. And if these messages didn't work, they wouldn't be financed by companies to push their products and their vision of the world. It is curious how marketing links products to natural impulses: the image of the car appears gliding down a narrow country road, with rivers, waterfalls, greenery – things that the corporations of manipulation know perfectly well to be powerful and authentic. But the end result will be another car, and millions of poor souls seated one behind the other in a traffic jam, usually reading billboards.

I think that we drastically underestimate the weight that is placed on our daily life by the individualization of how we meet our needs – the process of social atomization. The family in the corporate vision is the basic unit of consumption. The community is a waste. In the atomized social universe that has been created, the community has separated into families. The extended family, full of aunts and uncles, grandparents, unforgettable cousins, that healthy mess that we still find in less 'capitalized' worlds, was replaced by the nuclear family, with only parents and children. Since no one can stand the claustrophobic family environment that was created, couples separate. In the United States, only one quarter of homes have parents and children – the vast majority have isolated individuals, single-parent families, and so on. In each apartment or house in the suburbs, the same prosperity of a car, refrigerator, television, computer ... and the same solitude.

Since we are all simultaneously bombarded by a social image of success, those that can tolerate it maintain between husband and wife, and between parents and children, a semblance of civilized coexistence, replete with the hypocrisies that result not from the fact that people are naturally hypocrites, but from the simple power of the idyllic image that appears in every television show, every advertisement, every film, of young blonde parents loving each other and their two blonde offspring, and painting their lovely house with that *special* paint that makes it even whiter. This all generates a powerful sense of artificiality, and results in a solitary and unhappy humanity. The film *American Beauty*, although exaggerated and simplistic, reflects well this absurd world.

Human beings cannot be happy if their social existence is restricted to the nuclear family – which ends up collapsing – and the functional and all too often artificial relations of one's profession. What *American Beauty* reflects is an immense feeling of social asphyxiation, systematically imposed by a grotesque and senseless system of consumerist accumulation, and by the reduction of our complex necessities to economic choices.

For the solitary electronic masturbators that we try to reduce ourselves to, there is no space for sports, music, or the myriad forms of social life. An entire generation enters the world of the image, where the book has no further function. Sports no longer provide a form of leisure allowing any chubby kid or adult to run awkwardly after the ball with their neighbourhood buddies – now sports are something to be watched, sitting on the sofa, eating potato chips, seeing muscular and superb athletes making superb plays.

Music is no longer the local group playing over a beer at the corner – it is a CD that plays the marvellous Pavarotti or the indistinguishable bands on MTV, transmitted by earphone to a solitary jogger passing alone and quietly through the park, getting exercise. Sports become a solitary activity, as do music and sex. The public square is no longer a social space, and if we sit on the bench for a while, it's likely they will consider we have a problem, and if we are dark-skinned they will ask for our papers. The neighbourhood dance party doesn't exist any more, because every day we can get our fill of shapely young women dancing for us, enthusiastically gyrating just inches from the camera, imagining they are filling us with desire and pleasure. And we are surprised at the hundreds of thousands of young people who show up at open shows, seeking a feeling of togetherness.

The church itself – which we used to go to, if the truth be known, more to see the girls all dressed up than for the sacraments, but which is an important space for the construction of values, for spiritual expression – is turning into a process of electronic manipulation, because it is no longer rooted in the neighbourhood, the community, and people's daily lives.

Millions of men and women watch the night-time soap operas, which allow them to live through borrowed lives. Instead of seeking a partner, they dream of the adventures of their electronic idols. It is no longer a television show, it is your life – 'You Decide'. It's a borrowed life, a life you watch rather than live. It is a ubiquitous phenomenon. Millions of billboards and posters all over the world, on every corner, in every store, incessantly bombard us with images of nearly nude women, suggesting with an orgasmic look the immense happiness that will be ours if we buy a new domestic appliance. Can this permanent displacement of affective impulses to acquisitive behaviour really be innocent in terms of our daily happiness?

The pursuit of a qualitative radical change, involving a new culture of development and economic activity, is essential. Until now, progressive forces have concentrated on the greater productivity of their economic programme, or on greater redistributive justice. It is very difficult to redistribute when the culture of inequality permeates the very content of production and consumption. And if the mega-corporations create an idiotic world, should we redistribute the idiocy?

When cultural processes become the determining dynamic of economic processes, it is likely that we have to think more broadly about the alternatives to the culture being generated. What we are seeking, in fact, is an alternative civilization.

Winds of Change

Life doesn't need to be absurd. Corporations and private interests only make sense if they are at the service of a better life, and not if they put us at the service of their needs for accumulation, and still have the nerve to suggest that we should be thankful because they give us jobs.

We know that confronted with a tree-lined park in the middle of the city, a businessman is indignant that someone hasn't thought of building a shopping mall there. Another might envisage a parking lot, while the advertising agent would think it simply ridiculous that the people in the park don't go home where they can sit comfortably on their sofa and see beautiful images of distant parks, between advertisements. There is no evil in the process. They seek to maximize their returns, with considerable technical competence, and no intelligence of life. It is our task, as a society, to take the reins of social change, to leave our children a world that is less violent, less stupid, more humane.

I recently went to give a course in Recife. The same city centre where I worked in 1963 was undergoing a radical transformation. The buildings were restored to their original architectural splendour. The squares were clean, well-lit, tree-lined. The port is being opened to the public, and turned into a leisure area. The narrow streets of the old centre are now a profusion of bars and restaurants, with tables on the wide sidewalks, and the traffic diverted elsewhere. An orchestra played live music in the middle of the street, a large outdoor dance was bringing couples to rediscover their rhythm, excitement, laughter, and interest in each other. It goes on every night, so there is no need to wait for carnival once a year. A carnival which, by the way, is becoming more of a televised industry, more of something to watch, than an opportunity for the traditional widespread anarchy. In Recife, people no longer have to wait for TV-Globo to show them the carnival.

Despite the great media empires, thousands of communities all over the planet are creating community radio and television, which permit the promotion of local activities and events, serve to integrate the initiatives of a wide range of groups, and allow the production of programmes with children from their own neighbourhood, watched with great pleasure by families that recognize themselves in them. Marta Suplicy, the mayor of São Paulo, put local radios into the school system, to be managed with and by the kids. Is the global *novela* really so indispensable? The media magnates and the policies that govern communications in Brazil are well aware of the dangers of this trend, and regularly denounce the 'pirate radios', suggesting that airplane crashes are being caused by the communities that create instruments for communicative integration. In a world where 'anything goes' in the pursuit of money, you really can get away with anything.

Millions of people all over the world are abandoning private banks that serve the global mechanisms of speculation, and moving to community banks of different types, like the Grameen Bank in Asia or Portosol in Porto Alegre, which are emerging rapidly all over the planet. The state-owned Banco do Nordeste today is offering credit to small-scale producers, based only on the word of the borrower, and organized by hundreds of community credit agents who work in the more remote municipalities of the Northeast. Poor people keep their word, and the default rate is less than 2 per cent. Corporations, on the other hand, keep lawyers.

Millions of people all over the planet are starting to consume according to social and environmental criteria, avoiding products associated with child labour and agricultural chemicals, for example. The phenomenon has had such an impact that today thousands of companies are seeking to rebuild their reputations, fighting for the right to put a 'green seal' on their products or to qualify for the Abrinq Foundation's seal of approval for a child-friendly company, and responding to countless similar initiatives.

There is already a powerful movement of people who demand that the banks and investment companies where they place their savings withhold investment from companies that damage the environment, manufacture arms, or derive profits in other unethical ways. The organization Transparency International, which today works in 77 countries, managed to block World Bank financing to dozens of large companies because they used corrupt practices to obtain contracts. In France over 80 financial institutions run by civil society organizations offer options to make ethical use of personal savings. They are obliged by law to inform investors about the final destination of their money, and there are guarantees by government savings institutions to make people feel secure in this alternative form of investment, currently growing by 20 per cent a year. In the US, the ethical marketplace is already a trillion-dollar initiative.

Millions of senior citizens, often confined to an idle existence in apartments or houses, are discovering that they can, individually or organized in groups and associations, use the decades of useful life that remain to them in positive ways such as helping to manage the community, animating leisure and cultural spaces, supporting preventive health in the community or contributing to tree-planting programmes. They may not all have mastered the latest technologies, but most have an immense personal knowledge – an increasingly rare and valuable element – and any amount of time.

Initiatives like these are permitting a resurgence of local economic initiatives. Trapped for so long in the view that jobs would come from General Motors or some other multinational, or as political pay-offs from some corrupt politician, communities are discovering their potential for self-organization. Paul Singer, who has given us so much in terms of economic analysis, today has rolled up his sleeves and helps in the formation of cooperatives throughout Brazil, and is building a trend towards *economia solidária* in the policies of the Lula government. The mayors of the industrial municipalities on the periphery of Greater São Paulo organized a regional chamber designed to facilitate activities of small and medium-sized businesses, integrating the efforts of municipalities, companies, unions and various universities, in order to create a favourable environment for the development on this scale. Small businesses are different, because they are not the type of corporation that can come and go, create and destroy jobs, according to variations in interest rates in some distant country. Small businesses have an owner, neighbourhood and identity, and are not faceless companies. They close as well, but others open, and we do well to create climates favourable to their flourishing.

I once participated in an international meeting organized by UNICEF in the south of Italy. Hundreds of projects were presented in the area of urban renewal focused on children, who are also citizens. Many cities already have children's advisory boards, which are to be consulted about all the significant architectural projects affecting children. Some very practical lessons were learned, for example that 50 per cent of children don't understand traffic signs. As a result, signs are being redesigned with the participation of children, so that they can understand them. 'Safe pathways' are being marked on sidewalks and streets to facilitate the autonomous movement of children around the city. Under pressure from children's movements, frequently with the support of teachers' organizations, squares and parks that had been invaded by automobiles and made into parking lots are being reclaimed as real squares with benches, green space, water and areas for socialization and humanization.

It is not our purpose, in this brief study, to list the efforts being undertaken by people who are discovering what it means to be a person, to be part of a society, and to have rights. Or what it means to be a citizen, and not just a client. Anyone who has the interest can become part of the initiatives that exist today in practically all corners of the world. Whoever wants to learn about this will find a large number of studies, Internet sites and alternative publications. The movement is already planet-wide, although widely ignored by those who think that reality is what appears in the mainstream media.

The essential thing here is to show that the common citizen is not necessarily powerless. We can vote with our wallets when making purchases, with our savings when investing, with our voluntary labour when supporting the civil society organizations that are springing up all over. An impressive number of people prefer to earn a smaller salary in a civil society organization that is socially useful than spend their lives trying to show off an empty individual success.

The uneasiness that we feel is not necessarily caused by the left or right, the rich or poor, or by developed or developing countries. The uneasiness is civilizational, or cultural in the broadest sense of this term. Humanity has opened the box, and liberated fantastic technologies, immense scientific potentials. But humanity's needs remain prosaically human. To adapt technologies and economic potential to serve human needs is a simple and yet hugely complex task. This task doesn't demand more products, but more initiative and organization, more social intelligence. It is especially important to realize that it doesn't depend on waiting for a particular redemptive class or personality to come to power. In fact, it is likely that no different political power will emerge unless we build from the ground up a society that can recapture the reins of its own development.

The truth is that we need a minimum of balance. The system has managed to create a monstrous reality through its pathological fragmentation. We have managed to separate economic activity from its environmental, social and cultural effects. We isolate economic theory from philosophy and from the social and political sciences. We create a pathological persona – the one-dimensional technocrat centred on profit. And this persona, because of its own position in the mega-corporations of the planet, and because of the technologies it manages, has great power to wield over the system, if not always to change it.

The system dominated by money, by profit, by marketing and publicity has to rediscover its own foundations, in order to serve life, rather than us serving it. And economics, as a science, has to cease to be an obscene instrument of manipulation and justification of narrow interests, and place itself once again at the service of humanity.

It is not the spectre of the hammer and sickle that today haunts the mega-corporations of money, speculation and manipulation, and their eternal political cheerleaders. What they should fear is cultural rejection by a society that is fed up, wants something else, and is actively building other possibilities.

Epilogue

A nice word, 'epilogue'. Almost forgotten nowadays. But since this book seeks to shake up the exaggerated objectivity of science, and introduce the subjectivity of everyday experience, I add these final comments as a sort of rethinking of the above thoughts.

I like white cheese – the various kinds of fresh cheese, ricotta, whatever. On my small veranda, I grow oregano, rosemary, basil, green onions, parsley, pepper, things of that sort. I've always liked to eat well. On a good slice of Italian bread, I put cheese, a bit of oregano, basil, and a bit of fresh-ground black pepper. On top, a few grains of coarse salt. It doesn't cost a lot of effort or money, but it gives me great pleasure.

Of course, this attitude could irritate a businessman focused on economies of scale, efficiency and competitiveness. And in fact, the supermarket offers me the same white cheese with '*fines herbes*' (yes, in French), already prepared, 140 grams per unit, for the sum of a dollar and a half. But since the large cheese companies pay around 10 cents per litre of milk to the producers, the plastic dish must contain something like 5 cents worth of cheese and herbs. I don't feel good about paying more than a dollar for this. Most importantly, however, I don't need a company to fill me with prepackaged products to 'save me time'. I don't want to go through life racing to earn money in order to buy things to save me time. And it doesn't bother me to irritate this type of businessman.

Not everything can be made at home, and extremisms don't get you very far. Sometimes I like to put a few drops of olive oil on my cheese – olive oil that comes from Portugal, is prepackaged, and is worth what I pay. But lately, I'm using a fragrant olive oil from Giovinazzo, in the south of Italy, from a region I visited when I used to work on the trains. I like to know that this olive oil is from a cooperative, run by traditional families who understand everything about olives and oil.

The absurd philosophy that rules us fits in one paragraph. The dynamics of success suggest that if Mr Berlusconi or General Food hear about the appeal and quality of this oil, the cooperative of traditional families will be bought up by a large vegetable oil company that will introduce just-in-time production, replace the characteristic fragrance of the olive oil from this region by a milder flavour that appeals to the 'average consumer', and lay off the older producers who defend traditional forms of production. Efficient consultants who read Jack Welch's words, the ones that according to my son Alexander come *Straight from the Butt,* will introduce an efficient organization where people will kill themselves at work in a permanent climate of insecurity. Those who lose their jobs will be attended to by specialized personnel. To promote the new 'traditional' product, the corporation will implement an extensive advertising campaign where a 'typical' old Italian will appear in an old cap claiming that everything being done is 'traditional'. Big business may destroy what exists, but it is not stupid. We will have more oil and less pleasure.

The truth is that between cheeses, love and work, not necessarily in that order, I am reconstructing my life. From the initial shock, as a teenager, of seeing the miserable children in Recife, to the indignation that I feel today about the 11 million children that die every year in the world from ridiculous causes, there was a profound change, or perhaps a kind of coming back. It has been a long trip, from an emotional and angry vision, through the dry and sterile path of macroeconomic models, to rearticulate today a more informed, and most importantly more humane, vision. My indignation persists, and today I am convinced that the complex arguments that justify the postponement of a decent wage, of help for a hungry child, of a decent health service, essentially constitute shameful rationalizations for interests that make little sense, and which lead us to an all-embracing impasse.

Our entire society is organized around the competition paradigm, when even economic efficiency, not to speak of the quality of life, is ripe for collaboration. We are all supposed to become winners. I feel, frankly, like a winner when I can spend a morning with my children, or with my strong yet fragile wife, Fátima. Some time ago, on holiday in Toronto where my oldest son lived, we spent some time playing football on the grass. Toronto has a park every half dozen blocks, without shopping malls. You can enter without a membership card, without dressing up, without an obligatory uniform. Human beings have the same liberty to enter as the birds or dogs. There's no one handing out advertising flyers. And the field is not even shadowed by those huge women on billboards explaining what we should buy to feel happy. It is surrounded by real trees.

I, in my late fifties, despite a solid background as a football player (many decades ago), had to resort to various dirty tricks and subterfuges to knock over my boys, who manoeuvred around me without the slightest respect. After a time, dirty, out of breath and no doubt on the verge of a heart attack, I lay prostrate on the ground, looking at the huge sky above, feeling the cool grass below, and enduring in silence the curses of my frustrated sons. Moments of happiness like these, no one can take away. They're not like money. They are part of something that we are losing sight of – a thing called life.

The reconstructed mosaic, for me, doesn't prevent indignation and suffering. But it makes sense of it, because emotions are good and ethics essential, and because technique and technology exist to serve us; because by joining the fragments of life, whatever the fractures, the mosaic of life can be built back into a whole.

Suggestions for Further Reading

The things I have tried to say in this little book are simple, and I have resisted quoting authors on what is fairly obvious. But since my hope is that some people will be interested in learning more about some of the issues raised, I decided to write a brief commentary on books that open up horizons, and that I think are worth reading. In reality, one doesn't need to read too much. More important than reading a lot, nowadays, is spending more time in choosing carefully what we read.

Above all, I think it is good to look at the authors, flesh and blood people who open up new paths. Reading Galbraith, for example – books like *The Good Society* – is hugely stimulating. *An American Dilemma*, by Gunnar Myrdal, is another milestone of the last century, bringing together economic analysis and an ethical and cultural vision. Another great book which refuses to grow old is *Our Common Future*, a study coordinated by Gro Brundtland, which lays out in clear terms the huge dilemma of survival of the planet. An author who has stimulated me is David Korten, who wrote *When Corporations Rule the World*, and *The Post-Corporate World*, and who traces the complete circle between the uncontrolled power of mega-corporations and the alternatives that are emerging early in this century. Jeremy Rifkin's book on employment seemed a little oversimplified to me, but *The Age of Access* is very helpful for understanding new trends in the transformation of culture into a commodity. Similarly, a book by Lawrence Lessig, *The Future of Ideas,* opens up a whole avenue of information on the struggle for the freedom of ideas in the brave new world we are building. Hazel Henderson brought a fresh view to economics, showing in *Building a Win-Win World* that we can build progress without pushing others down, and that the formal economy actually represents only a relatively small part of our activities. Joel Bakan's book *The Corporation* is an excellent update on the problems of the corporate world, and the corresponding documentary in 2004 has become a landmark for the subject (www.thecorporation.tv). These different readings actually bring us the understanding of a deeper trend, the major shift from the competition paradigm to the collaboration paradigm in the overall understanding of economics.

But there is another way to find good reading, which is to keep abreast of the work of organizations that are doing cutting-edge research. Whoever wants more knowledge about the Third Sector, for example, can visit Johns Hopkins University by Internet, at the site http://jhu.edu or through the site http://rits.org.br, which is a network of information about the Third Sector in Brazil (Rede de Informações para o Terceiro Setor). The organization Pólis, an NGO based in São Paulo, has carried out research on the alternatives emerging with the growing role of civil society. The site is http://www.polis.org.br. The Abrinq Foundation has carried out extensive work around problems of the child, but is also developing new ways of organizing partnerships for a more humane society. In recent years emergent business organizations with ethical and humanitarian aims – Cives, Ethos, Gife, PNBE (Pensamento Nacional das Bases Empresarias) and others – have begun to identify very interesting paths to the construction of a new civic culture and a responsible business community. Municipalities all over the world are developing new, participatory and democratic forms of public administration: one can find innovative experiences in areas such as participatory budgeting, education, health and administration at the site http://web-brazil.com/gestaolocal, which brings together databases from CEPAM (Centro de Estudos e Pesquisas de Administração Municipal), Pólis, Abrinq, Snai-pt and Gestão Pública e Cidadania of the Fundação

Getúlio Vargas. It is important to note that civil society, because it is organized from the bottom up and in a very decentralized and widely dispersed manner, has relatively little visibility, but is a powerful movement that allows any person, in any city, to begin organizing to change something. I've mentioned some institutions here, not because they are the only or the most important ones, but to provide some initial points of contact in Brazil. And Brazil, curiously enough for a country so unequal and violent, is becoming an important source of social and political innovation. But similar links and connections can be found practically anywhere nowadays. The basic issue is that people are finding new ways of building another world, through fair trade, ethical finance, the non-monetary economy, community radio and televisions and the like, building new networks of solidarity. We tend to expect that the big, necessary changes will be brought about by other people, in another place. Not necessarily.

A third avenue to explore are the various international reports. One could once write more or less definitive books about the international situation. But with the current pace of change, a range of institutions have now started publishing annual reports, forming an invaluable instrument for keeping abreast of the planetary transformations. At the top of the list is the excellent *Human Development Report*, published annually by the UNDP, which can be obtained from any United Nations office or at the site http://hdr.undp.org. The *Human Development Report for Brazil* is an excellent research instrument for studying social dynamics in Brazil, especially the 1996 report, which was a methodological benchmark; it can be found at http://www.undp.org.br/HDR/Hdr96/rdhbin.htm. UNESCO publishes the *World Information and Communications Report*, with excellent studies of global transformations in the areas of information and educational technologies. UNCTAD's *World Trade and Development Report* presents excellent annual analyses of international economic trends, with a much more open perspective than the World Bank's well-established *World Development Reports*. The monthly publication *Le Monde Diplomatique*, also published in English, is one of the best sources of international information available today.

I would also like to mention a book of vast intelligence, *History of the World*, by J. M. Roberts. Reality today is changing at such a speed, and the media inundate us with so many new developments with no past and no future, that to recover a well-grounded and informed historical perspective has become essential. We have all been subjected to history when at school, usually with little profit. Going back to history at an adult age, when we have much more information and experience, is hugely enjoyable, and reconciles us with life. And Roberts's book is truly a work of genius.

But let us not forget the present author, who has produced various studies during his life. These are available at the site http://ppbr. com/ld, or http://dowbor.org, organized into articles, books, lines of research, and reading notes. The papers are free. Most are in Portuguese; some are in English, Spanish or French; a few in Polish. The site also has a message-board that allows the reader to communicate their interest or irritation, in a very democratic manner.

Index